New Directions for Student Services

John H. Schuh
EDITOR-IN-CHIEF

Elizabeth J. Whitt
ASSOCIATE EDITOR

Student Affairs Staff as Teachers

Emily L. Moore
EDITOR

Number 117 • Spring 2007
Jossey-Bass
San Francisco

STUDENT AFFAIRS STAFF AS TEACHERS
Emily L. Moore (ed.)
New Directions for Student Services, no. 117
John H. Schuh, Editor-in-Chief
Elizabeth J. Whitt, Associate Editor

NEW DIRECTIONS FOR STUDENT SERVICES (ISSN 0164-7970, e-ISSN 1536-0695) is part of The Jossey-Bass Higher and Adult Education Series and is published quarterly by Wiley Subscription Services, Inc., A Wiley Company, at Jossey-Bass, 989 Market Street, San Francisco, California 94103-1741. Periodicals Postage Paid at San Francisco, California, and at additional mailing offices. POSTMASTER: Send address changes to New Directions for Student Services, Jossey-Bass, 989 Market Street, San Francisco, CA 94103-1741.

New Directions for Student Services is indexed in College Student Personnel Abstracts and Contents Pages in Education.

Microfilm copies of issues and articles are available in 16mm and 35mm, as well as microfiche in 105mm, through University Microfilms Inc., 300 North Zeeb Road, Ann Arbor, Michigan 48106-1346.

SUBSCRIPTIONS cost $80 for individuals and $195 for institutions, agencies, and libraries in the United States. See ordering information page at end of book.

EDITORIAL CORRESPONDENCE should be sent to the Editor-in-Chief, John H. Schuh, N 243 Lagomarcino Hall, Iowa State University, Ames, Iowa 50011.

www.josseybass.com

CONTENTS

BICENTENNIAL
1807
WILEY
2007
BICENTENNIAL

THE WILEY BICENTENNIAL—KNOWLEDGE FOR GENERATIONS

*E*ach generation has its unique needs and aspirations. When Charles Wiley first opened his small printing shop in lower Manhattan in 1807, it was a generation of boundless potential searching for an identity. And we were there, helping to define a new American literary tradition. Over half a century later, in the midst of the Second Industrial Revolution, it was a generation focused on building the future. Once again, we were there, supplying the critical scientific, technical, and engineering knowledge that helped frame the world. Throughout the 20th Century, and into the new millennium, nations began to reach out beyond their own borders and a new international community was born. Wiley was there, expanding its operations around the world to enable a global exchange of ideas, opinions, and know-how.

For 200 years, Wiley has been an integral part of each generation's journey, enabling the flow of information and understanding necessary to meet their needs and fulfill their aspirations. Today, bold new technologies are changing the way we live and learn. Wiley will be there, providing you the must-have knowledge you need to imagine new worlds, new possibilities, and new opportunities.

Generations come and go, but you can always count on Wiley to provide you the knowledge you need, when and where you need it!

WILLIAM J. PESCE
PRESIDENT AND CHIEF EXECUTIVE OFFICER

PETER BOOTH WILEY
CHAIRMAN OF THE BOARD

Editor's Notes

The teaching role of student affairs professionals is increasing in importance as colleges and universities emphasize retention and graduation of undergraduates. Student affairs professionals play a crucial role in this process.

At Iowa State University, I have taught a very popular graduate course on college teaching with my former graduate assistant, Rebekah Marsh. Over time, we noticed growing enrollment among student affairs professionals. This pattern seemed to parallel the increased teaching roles of student affairs staff in the academy. As student affairs staff interest in our class grew, we became aware that many were finding themselves in more formalized teaching roles without sufficient expertise for their new and increasing responsibilities.

This volume reflects on the paradigm shift of student affairs staff from enablers to teachers. It addresses this phenomenon, beginning with a chapter framing the issues facing staff as they extend their informal teaching role outside the classroom into a more formal role inside the classroom.

In Chapter One, Rebekah S. Marsh and I examine the combination of the art and the act of teaching. We term this combination "teaching from near and far." Understanding the emphasis on student success, colleges are broadening the role of student affairs professionals in formal learning experiences. This chapter provides readers with the keys to successful teaching.

Mimi Benjamin, Kurt Earnest, Doug Gruenewald, and Ginny Arthur in Chapter Two address the many options, decisions, interactions, and individual and group activities that students deal with during the first weeks of college life. They particularly focus on this critical transitional period as one in which more intentional in-class and out-of-class experiences can be developed to enhance student learning.

Chapter Three provides an insider view on the mission and development of the First-Year Experience movement. Mary Stuart Hunter and Kathleen A. Murray discuss the influence of access and retention on the development of the movement as well as the importance of effective teaching to the success of the program.

Learning communities are explored in Chapter Four by authors Shari Ellertson and Karla V. Thoennes. They discuss the collaboration of academic affairs and student affairs in facilitating student learning and development in the learning community forum.

Chapter Five examines the often-discussed interaction of academic affairs and student affairs in a small college. This is a place where unique opportunities exist for staff to interact without boundaries. This chapter was

NEW DIRECTIONS FOR STUDENT SERVICES, no. 117, Spring 2007   © Wiley Periodicals, Inc.
Published online in Wiley InterScience (www.interscience.wiley.com) • DOI: 10.1002/ss.227

written by a faculty member, Greta Degen, and a student affairs professional, Erin Sheldahl, who work together to create student-focused learning on their campus.

Chapter Six introduces student affairs professionals to their part in the transformation of higher education programs that promote student learning and cocurricular settings. J. Herman Blake and I—with a combined academic career of more than fifty years of service across the range of four-year and two-year colleges and universities—provide practical strategies and understandings on how to articulate, communicate, and disseminate as scholarly practitioners.

In the last chapter, J. Herman Blake describes his successful efforts to build lower-division units on residential and commuter campuses where the teaching and learning integrate student affairs professionals into the academic programs. He uses his vast knowledge and experience to project readers into the future as student affairs staff teaching increases in the academy. Last, he challenges student affairs professionals to consider the wisdom of the African proverb "You don't build a house for yesterday's rains" in relation to effective and creative professionals with student affairs responsibilities.

I am grateful to the authors who have contributed to this volume. They provided substance and knowledge based on their research and work in the academy. I am also very proud to acknowledge that five of the authors are my former graduate students, and two of them were also teaching assistants. I am particularly honored to call them "my colleagues," and because of them my hope for the future soars.

I would also like to express special thanks to Thomas "Tony" King, executive assistant in the Office of the Provost at Dillard University, for his efforts in the completion of this volume.

I hope you find this sourcebook useful in your work.

Emily L. Moore
Editor

EMILY L. MOORE *is professor emerita of educational leadership and policy studies at Iowa State University. In January 2007 she was appointed provost and vice president for academic affairs at Dillard University in New Orleans, Louisiana.*

NEW DIRECTIONS FOR STUDENT SERVICES • DOI: 10.1002/ss

1

This chapter describes a new perspective on student learning and its impact on the act and art of college teaching. It also addresses the teaching role of student affairs professionals.

College Teaching for Student Affairs Professionals

Emily L. Moore, Rebekah S. Marsh

Student affairs professionals have a significant influence on early college experiences because they are the first contacts for incoming students. It has long been understood that these beginning interactions can promote early success or lay the foundation for student failure. With a view toward enhancing student success beyond the initial encounter, colleges are emphasizing the broader role of student affairs professionals in the formal learning experiences of their new charges. As a consequence it is important that we address the issue of student affairs staff as teachers in both formal and informal settings.

Student affairs professionals play an increasingly important role in formal and informal instruction, with greater emphasis on classroom learning. An awareness of the art as well as the act of teaching is paramount in staging the student's successful entrance into collegiate life. Furthermore, when they feel secure about what they teach and knowledgeable about how to adequately communicate with various student populations, student affairs professionals provide a stronger foundation for learning. In addition, understanding the dilemma created in fulfilling the "hands-on" helping role of student affairs (being near) and facilitating the "hands-off" teaching role of student affairs (being far) provides a learning dimension to the new student experience.

NEW DIRECTIONS FOR STUDENT SERVICES, no. 117, Spring 2007 © Wiley Periodicals, Inc.
Published online in Wiley InterScience (www.interscience.wiley.com) • DOI: 10.1002/ss.228

New Perspectives on Student Learning

The NASPA-ACPA publication *Learning Reconsidered* (Keeling, 2004) defined learning as "a comprehensive, holistic, transformative activity that integrates academic learning and student development, processes that have often been considered separate and even independent." It further explained that learning is more than "academic instruction, the acquisition of disciplinary content, or classroom learning" (p. 2). It is a concept that recognizes the many dimensions by which students are engaged in learning through cognitive understanding and personal development as well as the impact of various educators in their many roles. However, as noted in Hamrick, Evans, and Schuh (2002), historically student affairs staffs were seen as providers of services and facilitators of the learning process rather than in the central role of contributors.

The U.S. Department of Education's Study Group on the Conditions of Excellence in American Higher Education (1984) concluded that the following three processes were highly effective in student learning: (a) active involvement of students in the learning process; (b) high expectations of students; and (c) assessment and feedback to students. Similarly, the research of Claude Steele (1997) shows that academic commitment, combining a positive sense of self and identity with academic domains, improved student motivation for academic achievement. Blake and Moore (2004) expanded these processes for effective student learning to include (a) front-loading academic programs; (b) homogeneous and heterogeneous social opportunities; (c) student identity with academic achievement, and (d) academic cooperation and mutual support. Further, building on this knowledge, they developed an approach to academic achievement for underserved students. Utilizing the current data and their experience as administrators and faculty, their approach mandates a combined student affairs perspective with rigorous academic programs.

These are the concepts that many student affairs staff understand and traditionally use when assisting students who are facing the complexities and challenges of academic learning. However, in the classroom setting, student affairs staff are often seen as enablers: those who teach about survival in the academy and on the campus.

In referencing the perceptive work of R. D. Brown (1972), Hamrick, Evans, and Schuh (2002) acknowledge his notion of student affairs as central to the total learning experience, and that they warrant equal status with teaching faculty. Recognizing that varying patterns of interaction with students have consequences both in and outside the classroom, the more contemporary approaches consider student affairs staff as teachers who emphasize the learning that keeps students in school while stressing the concepts that advance students through college.

We refer to this approach as meeting our responsibilities to students by being "near and far." Thus, this chapter explains the act and the art of enhancing learning through the keys to successful teaching. This volume further reflects on the paradigm shift of student affairs staff from enablers to teachers.

The Art of Enhancing Learning

Richard Elmore defines teaching as "a messy, indeterminate, inscrutable, often intimidating, and highly uncertain task" (1991, p. ix). By contrast, teaching may also be carefully planned. The challenge for student affairs staff as teachers is to integrate both of these approaches into a seamless web of learning experiences for students.

We believe that teaching represents a singular commitment to future generations. Effective teaching requires passion and preparation; knowledge and subject mastery are summarized in a clear, concise, and well-written syllabus. We believe that each class session should communicate one's dedication to the education of one's students and their social development and intellectual learning. Each class offers student affairs staff practice in pedagogy and understanding what works best. Most importantly, they will learn firsthand how their excellence in the classroom enhances student learning.

In recent years, we find a growing number of student affairs staff taking our course on college teaching. Most of these individuals finish the course with a better understanding of and a greater appreciation for the knowledge base, commitment, work, and passion of their professors.

We know that the act of teaching is a complex and challenging task that assumes knowledge of the discipline and ability to communicate. We believe that these are necessary; however, standing alone, they are insufficient skills to effectively reach students. In our class, participants also learn that the art of teaching is a blend of student involvement, sensitivity, and wisdom engaged in the development and preparation of a future generation. We see the success of the combination of the act and the art of teaching, as Chickering and Gamson (1991) point out when students make what they learn part of themselves.

We believe that student affairs staff are intellectuals who bring an artist's perspective to a teaching environment. They enable and teach with knowledge and innovative creativity as a result of being near and far. The consequence is enhanced student learning.

The Qualities of a Craft: Becoming Artists

We believe that several issues are key to success in teaching: a well-developed philosophy of teaching; a clear syllabus; professionalism, authority, and approachability; student active engagement; and multiple forms of assessment and feedback. We use the syllabus as a foundation to reflect our beliefs about what teachers need to understand in creating an environment that conveys student learning. We apply theories in practical teaching situations to explore ways in which classroom experiences and environments enhance learning.

NEW DIRECTIONS FOR STUDENT SERVICES • DOI: 10.1002/ss

Philosophy of Teaching. The organizing principles of a course arise from one's philosophy of teaching. Instructors must first consider what they believe about education and how those beliefs affect their teaching. Second, they should consider how knowledge of the subject matter is developed in the discipline. For example, the philosophy of teaching of one of us, Emily Moore, reflects her beliefs about faculty responsibility and student learning:

> Faculty must stay informed about the changing population of students, as well as their interests and concerns. This involves effective communication with student groups and their leaders. As well, my philosophy is rooted in student learning. I believe that the expectation for student success should be high and achievable. Faculty should be as diligent in their teaching as students are diligent in their learning.
>
> I believe that students are the future. They are taught to achieve in a future that exceeds our comprehension of what will come. Their learning will provide for the success of the next generations. As an administrator and a teacher, I am responsible for providing the vision.
>
> The ultimate success of the institution depends on leadership that communicates, builds trust, provides structure, extends respect, makes the appropriate decisions, acknowledges problems, and promotes team efforts for the common good. [E. L. Moore, personal communication, Oct. 2005]

We require students in our course to write their philosophy of teaching. They must reflect on their own ideas, beliefs, and values about education, students, and teaching responsibility. They are required to begin the opening statement with "I believe."

We realize that, for some student affairs staff, this may be the first time they have reflected on the principles and values that motivate them as a foundation for their teaching. Thus, personalizing these beginning thoughts and statements provides greater ownership of and responsibility for the impact of their philosophy on students. They will continue to refine their ideas through maturity, study, and experience in teaching.

Syllabus. We strongly believe that the syllabus is an informative agreement between the professor and the student and is crucial in setting the stage for the students' learning. It sets a tone for the class, telling students what they can expect of their instructor and what he or she expects of them.

The syllabus is an outline of the course of study. It must be well-written with concise statements providing students with a clear understanding of learning expectations and goals, policies, procedures, dates of assignments, grades, and evaluation and assessments. It should assist students with insights and appreciation for the discipline and the subject matter.

The syllabus should demand rigor and challenge students to seek new levels of excellence. High expectations and respect for students' minds should be apparent in the syllabus. It is an important document that should be read with the class on the first day. Questions about it should be asked and answered.

The instructor should refer students to the syllabus as a guide throughout the semester. If the instructor is considering changes in requirements in the syllabus, clear communication of those changes is imperative. Often we provide students with a written update of the syllabus with explanation, if a change is needed. The operative words are "clear communication."

Students often grumble and complain about the rigor of the work expected of them. They may even challenge the selection of materials. Students will, however, accept the requirements. This acceptance develops because of the instructor's consistency in the written syllabus and in his or her actions, clear communications with them, and an obvious respect for their learning.

A well-written syllabus is the first step in classroom management. If the instructor cannot manage the class, the environment will not be conducive to learning. The syllabus provides the strength and the substance for the course. However, the instructor makes it work.

Professionalism, Authority, and Approachability. In our experience, what "makes it work" is effective teaching, requiring professionalism, authority, and approachability. These are all forms of classroom management. According to Nilson (1998), at the university level managing a classroom pertains more to maintaining an orderly environment for learning than to disciplinary concerns. The instructor commands class attention and models acceptable behavior through his or her professionalism, authority, and approachability. Professionalism includes presentation of self: dress, voice, respectful demeanor. Classroom authority is shown by presentation of skills: knowledge and command of content, organization of presentation, use of language, and delivery of the message. Students become restless and lose attention when they are uninterested and bored. Practicing these presentation skills assists an instructor in maintaining students' interest (Nilson, 1998).

Approachability is shown through many techniques, including the instructor's office hours; projection of personal confidence, conviction, and warmth regarding student learning; cooperation without antagonism; and maintaining integrity and composure while not accepting disruptive behavior or verbal abuse.

We have learned that teaching students as we would want to be taught ourselves and modeling appropriate behavior in class will create an environment in which students are more likely to approach us. The instructor is, in essence, developing in the classroom a sense of community.

For example, our class on college teaching met on the evening of the American national tragedy of September 11, 2001. Among the eighteen students were eleven Americans and seven international students heralding from Asia, Latin America, and Eastern Europe. Our primary objective for this class session was to discuss the ways in which an instructor could incorporate such a national tragedy and emotional event into her teaching. The discussion was to center on how to incorporate our lesson and support our students during this time of great sorrow. However, the actual class outcome was very different from what we had anticipated or planned.

As students began presenting their teaching perspectives it quickly became apparent that the emotions of the event were ruling the discussion. Without instructor intervention, the international students began to comfort the American students and the instructors. They spoke about their own countries, their daily living experiences, their happiness and their fears, and most importantly, their belief that a better world is achievable. They knew firsthand about tragedy, war, and battles, yet they believed in the resiliency of the human spirit. They felt our collective grief and knew how to comfort us.

We all gained much more than we expected that evening. However, the true lesson of learning would not have occurred without a previous environment of respect, modeling of behavior, and approachability among the students and instructors.

Student Engagement. Student engagement means active involvement in the learning experience rather than passive listening. In a study of college students' intellectual development cited by Hamrick, Evans, and Schuh (2002), Baxter Magolda suggested that it is most desirable to use teaching strategies that create an active classroom, including student discussion and connecting real-life activities to the classroom.

Active involvement in the learning experience includes reading assignments, leading discussions, and participating in study groups. These requirements are designed to maximize the amount of time students spend learning outside of the classroom and their ability to participate inside of the classroom. The goal is to increase the amount of time on task. Because of classroom expectations, students have to put in more time outside of the classroom.

In another course students were required to develop poster presentations that were displayed in the hall for faculty and peer review. The theme and idea of the poster were based on classroom readings, reflection, and discussion. The students designed and discussed the posters alone, without directions from the instructor. Students learned, sometimes unwillingly, skills and competencies consistent with the activity, such as researching, writing, communication, oral presentation, and development of a more in-depth knowledge base (Kuh, 2001; Astin, 1993).

The goal was that, over time, the articulation process of reading, reflection, and discussion, integrated with the analysis of the literature, would lead to greater understandings and insights. Often found in scholarly conferences, poster presentations can enhance teaching and learning.

Assessment and Feedback. Narrative evaluations of student performance, written commentaries on paper, and other assignments are important assessment and feedback strategies. Anything that increases interaction between the instructor and the student can become a feedback mechanism. The goal is for the student to look beyond the class as a series of tests and instead focus on learning.

NEW DIRECTIONS FOR STUDENT SERVICES • DOI: 10.1002/ss

Changing students' self-concepts and awareness of themselves as learners is difficult. Many have been taught in an environment in which they think of courses and learning as a series of tests. They must understand that assessment really is interaction with the instructor and the work—the critical responses from student peers and the narrative evaluations of student work. Students should get immediate feedback on their academic work.

By contrast, an instructor also may employ a timely strategy of learning by encouraging students to develop their own understandings through self-assessment. In other words, instructors should not "hold students' hands" through a project by providing all the details and directions for them to follow.

Instructors should allow students the freedom to make decisions. The feedback from the instructor may be minimal, but the support is maximal. The poster requirement in one of our classes, mentioned earlier, often precipitated a response of reticence, a desire for more guidance. For some students, the journey seemed wretched.

The poster project was based on the students' research of an issue affecting them. They were required to complete a comprehensive essay and then prepare a conference-quality poster that summarized the paper and demonstrated the saliency of the issue selected.

Initially, students wanted more detailed information and direction. They felt the instructor was not providing enough information to complete the project or enough constructive feedback as they developed their posters and themes. They were fearful of making their own decisions about the project. When more instruction was not forthcoming, the reaction from some individuals was despair and even anger.

We believe that student engagement includes respect for students' minds and abilities. It involves giving them the opportunity for self-learning. From our perspective, every poster did not have to be the same size or provide the information in the same manner or have similar themes. Every poster simply needed to provide information, show creativity, and communicate to the viewer the issue addressed and the outcome.

At the completion of the project, students were asked to orally assess the experience. They critically evaluated their assumptions and realized their positive experience and significant change. The awareness that they had the abilities to analyze and make decisions based on their own research and understandings of an issue was a priceless learning experience.

The Impact of Teaching: Near and Far

Education, it has been stated, is not complete until students have both acquired knowledge and the ability to act on that knowledge in the world (Colby, Erlich, Beaumont, and Stephens, 2003). How does the what, the why, and the how of what one teaches affect students' futures? As stated earlier, success is seen when students make what they learn a part of themselves.

J. Herman Blake's philosophy of learning reflects his belief about students as well as his belief about the impact of teaching. "There is no known limit to the capacity of the human mind to learn, develop, grow, and change" (J. H. Blake, personal communication). There are no limits to the capacity of the mind to learn. There are no age, gender, race, or ethnic limits or any other parameters we may use to define ourselves or others. In the process of teaching and learning, we must challenge ourselves to achieve above our limits. It is our responsibility to engage and encourage our students to realize goals beyond their perceived limits and further.

Awareness that what one says and does has an impact far beyond the fifty minutes of class is central to student learning and the instructor's own understanding of teaching. Keith Karnok (2001) indicates that the teacher who works with students to reach their full potential and cares about them will have the most lasting effect on students.

Over time, new instructors realize the impact of their teaching, near and far, as former students return with stories of new experiences and unexpected but positive outcomes because what they brought to the classroom was integrated into what they learned, and it opened new and creative vistas to them.

Student affairs professionals as teachers offer the near and far of teaching—a new and exciting paradigm for higher education.

References

Astin, A. W. *What Matters in College? Four Critical Years Revisited.* San Francisco: Jossey-Bass, 1993.

Blake, J. H., and Moore, E. L. "Retention and Graduation of Black Students: A Comprehensive Strategy." In I. M. Duranczak and others (eds.), *Best Practices for Access and Retention in Higher Education.* Minneapolis: Center for Research on Developmental Education and Urban Literacy, University of Minnesota, 2004.

Brown, R. D. *Student Development in Tomorrow's Higher Education: A Return to the Academy.* Student Personnel Series no. 16. Washington, D.C.: American Personnel and Guidance Association, 1972.

Chickering, A. W., and Gamson, Z. (eds.). *Applying the Seven Principles for Good Practice in Undergraduate Education.* San Francisco: Jossey-Bass, 1991.

Colby, A., Ehrlich, T., Beaumont, E., and Stephens, J. *Educating Citizens: Preparing America's Undergraduates for Lives of Moral and Civic Responsibility.* San Francisco: Jossey-Bass 2003.

Elmore, R. R. "Foreword." In C. Roland Christensen, David A. Garvin, and Ann Sweet (eds.), *Education for Judgment.* Boston: Harvard Business School Press, 1991.

Hamrick, F. A., Evans, N. J., and Schuh, J. H. *Foundations of Student Affairs Practice.* San Francisco: Jossey-Bass, 2002.

Karnok, K. J. "Thoughts on College Teaching." In F. Stephenson (ed.), *Extraordinary Teachers: The Essence of Excellent Teaching.* Kansas City: Andrews McMeel, 2001.

Keeling, R. (ed.). *Learning Reconsidered: A Campus-Wide Focus on the Student Experience.* Washington, D.C.: National Association of Student Personnel Administrators and American College Personnel Association, 2004.

Kuh, G. "College Students Today: Why We Can't Leave Serendipity to Chance." In P. G. Altback and others (eds.), *In Defense of American Higher Education.* Baltimore: Johns Hopkins University Press, 2001.

Nilson, L. B. *Teaching at Its Best*. Bolton, Mass.: Anker, 1998.

Steele, C. "A Threat in the Air: How Stereotypes Shape Intellectual Identity and Performance of Women and African Americans." *American Psychologist*, 1997, *52*, 613–629.

U.S. Department of Education, Study Group on the Conditions of Excellence in American Higher Education. *Involvement in Learning: Realizing the Potential of American Higher Education*. Washington, D.C.: National Institute of Education, 1984.

EMILY L. MOORE is professor emerita of educational leadership and policy studies at Iowa State University. In January 2007 she was appointed provost and vice president for academic affairs at Dillard University in New Orleans, Louisiana.

REBEKAH S. MARSH is a postdoctoral research associate in the Department of Human Nutrition at Ohio State University.

2

At the beginning of the first year, student affairs staff members serve as educators through special programs and activities that have an impact on students' success in college.

The First Weeks of the First Year

Mimi Benjamin, Kurt Earnest, Doug Gruenewald, Ginny Arthur

Institutions of higher learning can be described as webs of learning opportunities both formal and informal. As committed participants in the educational process, student affairs professionals must be attentive to the web's effectiveness. Cohen, Raudenbush, and Ball (2002) suggest that it is incumbent upon educators to pay attention to the interrelated factors, such as educational goals and content, learner characteristics, educator characteristics, and interactions with the learner in context, to determine how to best meet the needs of today's students. Similarly, King (2003) notes, "When these [factors] are mutually reinforcing (or 'in alignment'), the potential for students to achieve educational goals is greatly enhanced" (p. 235). The evidence is convincing that learning occurs in a context.

That context is complex and multifaceted, with activity occurring in the classroom and the laboratory as well as in the residence halls and the student union. Many individuals play a role in the educational process, including faculty, administrators, staff members, and students. Faculty members usually are responsible for delivering content material in the classroom, whereas student affairs educators provide learning experiences throughout the campus. Blimling and Alschuler (1996) note, "We contend that student development educators are teachers with a mission as clear as faculty members' devotion to their disciplines" (p. 203). By promoting "self-knowledge, and the intellectual, cultural, and personal development of students" (p. 208), they contribute to students' learning experiences and serve as teachers in the college or university context.

New Directions for Student Services, no. 117, Spring 2007   © Wiley Periodicals, Inc.
Published online in Wiley InterScience (www.interscience.wiley.com) • DOI: 10.1002/ss.229

As student affairs professionals strive to maximize the educational experiences of students, we must focus on the contexts in which learning occurs. It is essential that we refine our approaches and identify reasonable points of overlap with our academic partners. Examining the early opportunities available to students entering postsecondary institutions is a logical first step. Focusing on this critical transition period provides university personnel with a multitude of possibilities to develop more intentional in-class and out-of-class experiences that enhance student learning.

This chapter addresses the important experiences of new college and university students during the first weeks of the first semester. These weeks are filled with interactions with other students in class, residence halls, dining centers, and student unions. They are filled with questions that include, "Will I like my roommate?" "Do I want to join a sorority-fraternity?" "Where is my calculus class?" Students have many options, and we explore the variety of opportunities, individuals, and activities that are available to them in the first few weeks.

One important caveat here: much of the information in this chapter is based on our collective experience, which is primarily in public, residential institutions. Differences may exist at community colleges, non-residential institutions, virtual campuses, and the like. Our hope is that professionals at all institutions will be able to translate this information, as appropriate, to their institutions.

Benefits of Involvement and Engagement

The terms *involvement* and *engagement* are commonly used to describe desirable situations or circumstances for students to experience during college. Astin's (1984) theory of student involvement suggests that active participation by students in their academic and personal experiences leads to learning and development. According to Kuh, Kinzie, Schuh, Whitt, and Associates (2005), "What students *do* during college counts more in terms of what they learn and whether they will persist in college than who they are or even where they go to college" (p. 8). Given the amount of time students spend outside the classroom, what they do often involves programs and activities coordinated by student affairs professionals.

Students experience multiple benefits from participation and engagement. They may benefit from experiential learning opportunities, such as a science major working in a laboratory as a research assistant or a marketing major serving as the public relations chair of a campus organization. These opportunities not only provide tangible experiences but also position these students to have contact with other "teachers," such as the faculty member who runs the lab, the club advisor, and peers involved in these activities. In addition, this interaction with knowledgeable others furthers students' academic and personal development. Because peer interactions exert significant influence (Astin, 1993), activ-

NEW DIRECTIONS FOR STUDENT SERVICES • DOI: 10.1002/ss

ities that involve students with their peers offer particularly ripe opportunities for learning.

The joint report entitled *Powerful Partnerships: A Shared Responsibility for Learning* (American Association for Higher Education, American College Personnel Association, and National Association of Student Personnel Administrators, 1998) suggests that learning is fundamentally about making and maintaining connections. Furthermore, the report comments that learning is an active search for meaning by the learner and suggests learners reach their greatest potential when they actively participate in the construction of knowledge. As students matriculate through colleges and universities, they make curricular and developmental connections and are given opportunities to expand their knowledge. Some points of connection are obvious. For example, students select courses that prepare them to reach their career aspirations. Faculty organize and sequence curricula in meaningful patterns that help students integrate ideas and themes and apply knowledge across courses and disciplines. Other points of connection are far less obvious and at times occur seemingly by accident. Experiences in the student affairs curriculum, such as leadership or community service, may not appear connected to students and may not be designed as intentionally as they could be for maximum learning to occur (Keeling, 2004). Therefore, it is essential to plan intentional, holistic experiences for new students during the first few weeks of the semester.

Location of Activities

The classroom is only one context for educational experiences. Additional opportunities for student affairs professionals to enrich students' learning environments occur in "student living, social, recreational, cultural, and spiritual settings—all of which can serve as natural and extended neoclassrooms, and all of which can help student affairs practitioners reach rapprochement with the faculty and contribute to the reintegration of the college" (Bloland, Stamatakos, and Rogers, 1996, p. 219). For the student development educator, teaching can take place in many settings, including student organization offices, the health and wellness center, the recreational services facilities, and the residence halls, as well as in the classroom (Blimling and Alschuler, 1996). Students gain valuable experiences working on campus (Astin, 1993), through service learning and community service activities in the community, and through their casual conversations in the dining hall or the campus commons. These types of activities and interactions are most significant to the learning experience (Terenzini, Pascarella, and Blimling, 1996).

Role of Student Affairs Educators

Although student affairs educators are usually categorized as "staff" and not "faculty," their role in students' academic success is imperative. Their work may include "organizing workshops, counseling individuals, advising organizations, and . . . creating educationally rich living environments that focus the influence of the peer environment on educational outcomes" (Blimling and Alschuler, 1996, p. 206). These educators teach students how to work in teams, manage time, have effective conversations, and make appropriate choices. King and Baxter Magolda (1996) identified sensitivity to the developmental issues that underlie the process of education as a strength of student affairs. They emphasized the importance of intentional learning goals and assessment of students' abilities, recommending the integration of cognitive and affective aspects of development through student affairs work.

It is also common for "teachable moments" to emerge, providing additional opportunities for student affairs educators who may see students in less structured environments than faculty. These unplanned learning experiences are important for staff to identify so that students can become more intentional about their involvement and reflection. An intentional approach will ideally lead to greater complexity of thought and action (Bloland, Stamatakos, and Rogers, 1996).

Importance of the First Few Weeks

Taking time at the beginning of the academic year to start educating new students through student affairs programs and services makes a difference. In the Developing Effective Educational Practice (DEEP) study of colleges and universities, Kuh, Kinzie, Schuh, Whitt, and Associates (2005) concluded that an effective strategy used by these institutions is "front-loading" resources to help students learn how to succeed as independent and interdependent learners. Because involvement often leads to integration in the community, a factor that Tinto (1993) identified as critical to retention, early involvement may lead to earlier integration.

The first weeks of school are a time to help new students deal with basic needs and adjustment issues, such as finding classes, changing schedules, and dealing with feeling overwhelmed. A variety of common activities aims to provide information to students so that they can make the kinds of choices that will lead to their success.

Common Activities During the First Weeks

These first weeks of school are critically important for new student adjustment. Prior to students' arrival on campus, sophisticated Web sites allow them to visit their residence hall rooms and campus buildings, giving them some familiarity with the campus. These experiences answer some of their logistical questions, but the more complex questions are answered through the programs, activities, and services provided before classes start, during those first few weeks.

NEW DIRECTIONS FOR STUDENT SERVICES • DOI: 10.1002/ss

Orientation. Fall orientation (also known as New Student Days, or Welcome Week on some campuses) is an increasingly important time for schools to make critical connections with new students. For many traditional-age college freshmen, the start of school can be a time of tremendous stress and upheaval in their lives. They are leaving the security and structure of home and starting a new life adventure. The student affairs mission is to help them with their social and emotional needs, physical needs, spiritual lives, and new academic life.

Consideration of the unique characteristics that students bring to the academy can result in special orientation programs designed to meet the needs of specific populations. For example, first-generation students may face additional adjustment challenges. Arizona State has addressed this institutional need by offering a special program at orientation designed for these students. Participating students and their families learn success tips, become familiar with university resources, and learn the benefits of a college degree. In addition, the program acknowledges and celebrates cultural heritage (National Resource Center for The First Year Experience and Students in Transition, 2005). Other institutions provide programming that targets students of color, commuters, international students, high-ability students, or residence hall students. Greek systems develop special programming for students who choose to become sorority or fraternity members. Offices of institutional research can play a critical role in identifying the preentry characteristics of students to inform the development of programs and services that maximize opportunities for all students to be successful.

Another special orientation program is designed for international students. Although all students have adjustments to make during their first year in college, there are added issues for students from other countries. Challenges may involve adjustments to culture, language, food, and living conditions. Universities have recruited students to come a great distance for an education and have a responsibility to ensure that such students receive an appropriate orientation to their new environment. The University of Wisconsin-Madison is one of many institutions that support international students with a separate orientation program as well as specific programs throughout the year.

A common model that an increasing number of schools are using to help first-year students is an experiential learning program at a camp or retreat prior to the start of classes. These programs, which are usually voluntary, take students off campus for one to five days. Programs such as "Dawg Camp" at the University of Georgia, "Frog Camp" at Auburn University, and "Launch" at Washington University introduce students to institutional traditions, leadership skills, and involvement opportunities. Vanderbilt University expands this type of program by offering a choice of five camp experiences for students to select from: traditional camp, intense outdoor adventures, leadership, multicultural, and service learning (National Resource Center for The First Year Experience and Students in Transition, 2005).

NEW DIRECTIONS FOR STUDENT SERVICES • DOI: 10.1002/ss

Service Programs. Service programs are popular at institutions such as Miami University (Ohio), Davidson College, and Wright State University. These programs introduce students to the local community, which can be particularly important for students on a "commuter" campus. Such programs give new students a purpose and focus while helping them acclimate to their new environment. In the process, they meet other students, faculty, and staff and begin to connect and bond with their new home (National Resource Center for The First Year Experience and Students in Transition, 2005).

Convocation. A number of campuses provide a "convocation" for new students. Often a formal presentation of an academic nature is provided along with symbolic activities through which messages about the institution and the students' connection to the institution are conveyed. Mount Holyoke College and Carlton College each have convocations, with Carlton scheduling weekly convocation events. This is an opportunity to officially welcome new students and set a tone for the year. It is a time for faculty and student affairs staff to begin to challenge students and set expectations for their success at the institution. Such programs can serve as important rituals for students—symbolic events that communicate to them that they are now official members of the community, and with their new rights come responsibilities for making their campus a better place.

Common Reading Programs. Many colleges assign new students common readings during the summer preceding entry. These are often connected to a first-year experience program. Such readings provide a common experience for students. They form a basis for discussion in English classes, learning communities, or orientation classes. Some institutions structure these programs to include discussion with professional staff or faculty members before classes start. Common reading programs exist at institutions such as Kalamazoo College, University of North Carolina-Chapel Hill, and Appalachian State College.

Residential Experiences and Learning Communities. Learning communities are yet another way in which students learn and student affairs staff members have an opportunity to teach. Pascarella, Terenzini, and Blimling (1994) indicated that residential living during college is consistently one of the most important determinants of student involvement or integration into the systems of an institution. Tinto (1993) noted that residence halls provide scaled-down environments that enable "newcomers to find an early physical, social, and academic anchor during the transition to college life" (p. 125). Pascarella (1985) contended that the influence of residential living persists even when controls are made for differences in students' precollege characteristics such as aptitude, extracurricular involvement, and socioeconomic status. These studies support long-held notions in the field of student affairs that residential living experiences significantly enhance student involvement and thus contribute positively to educational attainment. Student affairs professionals can build on these findings by dialoguing about and assessing the factors that strengthen academic integration and then developing living-learning environments that intentionally maximize opportunities for students to engage in the construction of knowledge and provide a context for such engagement to occur with regularity.

The learning community initiatives that have emerged across the country over the last two decades, such as those at the University of Michigan, University of Missouri-Columbia, University of Oregon, and The Evergreen State College, are sterling examples of the educational advancements that can be achieved when college and university personnel come together to discuss how architectural structures, curricular adjustments, and staffing considerations increase opportunities for student achievement. They demonstrate the potential that exists when academic and student affairs professionals enter into partnerships that willingly blur the lines between the two cultures in an effort to maximize learning.

In many ways, such initiatives capitalize on the varied contexts in which students learn and result in paradigm shifts regarding the types of environments that support student learning. Grouping students based on academic interests, working to increase student and faculty interaction outside the classroom, and pedagogical innovations are all hallmarks of learning community programs. In the example of residence halls, we see that student affairs professionals have demonstrated a willingness to consider how residence hall facilities, assignment processes, and staffing patterns can contribute to educational purposes previously reserved for the academicians.

A Sample Curriculum

Iowa State University, like other institutions, provides many opportunities for new students to become involved and engaged. What follows is a brief chronological overview of the types of activities that students are encouraged to experience. This "curriculum" for new students is continually evolving, and reflects the ISU culture. When developing programs, the institutional culture and the types of students for whom the activities are designed must be taken into consideration. The Iowa State model is offered simply as one example of the many ways in which students can be exposed early on to the "other" teachers available to assist them with their transition to the university and help them build learning connections. Information about each program is available on the Iowa State University Web site (http://www.iastate.edu).

The culture at Iowa State is decentralized. Each college, division, and department is encouraged to be entrepreneurial as well as collaborative. Hence, there are many opportunities available to students, some of which are connected to one another and many of which stand alone. In general, the goals of these activities are similar:

• To welcome new students, help them navigate the institution, and feel a sense of belonging

- To provide information about how to get involved and invitations to do so
- To make a large institution "feel" small and personal

Generally, the first program of this type that students experience is orientation. There are orientations designed for traditional-age new students, transfer students, international students, and students of color.

The orientation for traditional-age students and transfer students takes place during the summer and is designed to help students find out what it's like "to BE a student at Iowa State . . . and to make sure you're ready to go on the first day of class!" (Iowa State University, 2007a). Students attending orientation participate in typical new student activities, including meeting with an academic advisor, registering for classes, and learning what the campus has to offer.

Incoming freshman students of color have the option of enrolling in an eight-week summer orientation program called the Academic Program for Excellence (APEX). In addition to taking courses, APEX students meet with faculty and staff who assist them with their transition to life at Iowa State University.

International student orientation is held the week before classes begin. The purpose of this program is to help international students make the transition to Iowa State. Meeting other students and staff, taking placement exams, and familiarizing themselves with U.S. customs and laws are central components of this program.

As new students arrive on campus, many efforts are made to help them connect and feel part of the community. Students interested in joining a sorority have the opportunity to participate in new member recruitment (fraternities recruit during the summer). Residence hall students are greeted by members of the "Move-In Crew." Over four hundred students, staff, and faculty volunteer to meet students and their families as they arrive to move into the residence halls and help them unload their belongings, carry them to their rooms, and help them get settled. Residence hall student government members volunteer at welcome stations, where they dispense information, advice, and cookies and beverages. Residence hall staff members check students into their rooms, and members of the university administration, including the president and vice president for student affairs, interact informally with students and families. The message here is that ISU is a friendly community, where people are available and accessible to help students succeed.

Also during this time, students of color are invited to participate in the Community Of Color Orientation (COCO), a three-day event for first-year ethnic students of various backgrounds that focuses on issues of "identity development, community building, and cultural transition" (Iowa State University, 2007b). Later in the semester, multicultural student affairs coordinates the Student of Color Convocation (SoCC) ceremony that officially welcomes students of color. This event is attended by the president, academic deans, faculty, staff, and students and conveys that students of color are an integral part of this institution and that their academic success is paramount.

Another program, Frontiers of the Discipline, occurs during the week preceding classes. Frontiers was piloted by the College of Liberal Arts and Science (LAS) in 2005. Seventy-five first-year students discussed cutting-edge issues in small groups with faculty. The groups met periodically throughout fall semester, attending lectures, special events, and discussions together. The intent of this program was to expose students immediately to current issues in a stimulating environment and give them a taste of future career options. Although Frontiers of the Discipline is currently facilitated solely by faculty, it is a good example of a program that could be enhanced by collaboration with student affairs staff. The learning experience could be extended into the residence halls, Greek houses, or student union by partnering with student affairs staff who could guide discussions during meals or evening hours.

All new students are encouraged to register for Destination Iowa State. This program is held several days before classes begin and is designed to help students feel welcome and a part of the ISU community. Faculty and student affairs staff are paired up with small groups of students to visit and talk about academic success. Activities are designed to help students learn how to navigate the campus and where to go for assistance. In the process, students meet classmates. Students who live in the residence halls participate in some of the activities with their house (or floor) mates, and the first house (or floor) meeting is part of the Destination Iowa State schedule of events. At this meeting, community assistants explain the roommate contract and encourage students to talk with their roommates about who they are and what is important to them in a living environment.

Additional activities offered during Destination Iowa State include a community improvement service project, which helps students see themselves as part of the larger Ames/ISU community and value the concept of "giving something back"; social events designed to encourage students to meet one another and interact with student leaders; and educational sessions that help students develop skills to be successful at Iowa State.

Several other campuswide programs occur during the first week of classes, or shortly thereafter. Over thirty-five hundred students attend WelcomeFest, where area businesses and organizations are invited to showcase their products and services. WelcomeFest offers a festival-like atmosphere that is appealing to the students. It also gives students an opportunity to peruse bank, grocery, entertainment, and other service options in the community. Students may find a job opportunity or simply enjoy the free food and the fun environment. Similarly, ClubFest is a convenient way for students to explore over 160 organizations while at the same time providing those organizations with a way to recruit new members. Organization members staff their tables in order to answer questions that prospective members may have.

During the first week of classes, student affairs staff, faculty, and administrators are available at welcome booths that are intentionally placed at several high-traffic locations on campus. Students are greeted as they make their way to classes and offered information about class locations, academic schedules, and how to decipher the campus bus schedule, and are given candy and beverages. Students tend to respond with slightly surprised pleasure at the unexpected attention and care, and faculty and staff have the opportunity to establish new connections with one another.

Although none of the preceding three programs is academic in nature, each demonstrates elements of the institutional climate that are essential to student success: accessibility of administrators and faculty, the importance of student involvement and peer leadership, and the connections between the university and the community.

Student affairs staff also provide more traditional academic support throughout the first semester. Residence hall directors and graduate students in psychology and educational leadership and policy studies teach Psychology 131. This one-credit-hour course sponsored by the Academic Success Center in the dean of students office focuses on learning issues and includes a variety of reading and study strategies and tactics, from time management to test taking. Class size is limited to twenty students to allow for group interaction as well as individual attention. Topics include time, memory, reading, notes, tests, diversity, thinking, writing, relationships, and health.

Supplemental Instruction (SI), also coordinated by the Academic Success Center, is available for students who are enrolled in select difficult 100- to 200-level courses. SI begins the second week of classes and provides regularly scheduled study sessions facilitated by SI leaders—undergraduate students who have previously taken the course and demonstrated academic competency in the subject area.

Residence hall "challenges" are another method of encouraging students to get involved with their peers around social and academic issues. The hall staff and student government collaborate in designing a challenge program that is unique to their residence hall. Most of the challenge programs begin during the first few weeks of the semester and continue until the end of the semester or academic year. Students are invited to participate in a variety of activities in order to win points, or "study bucks," which can be redeemed for prizes and which will contribute to their house (or floor) total points. The house with the highest number of points wins the challenge. Students can get points for attending lectures, performances, or campus events; showing their hall directors an A or B paper; being seen studying; and participating in intramurals or hall activities. Houses also get points for meeting or exceeding the goal they set for their house GPAs. These challenge programs have been very popular and have succeeded in getting students involved and establishing an academic environment in the residence halls.

The programs described here are a sampling of the activities designed for new Iowa State students to experience as they become accustomed to their new environment. Students respond positively, and comments indicate that the programs achieve the general goals identified earlier. True to the Iowa State decentralized culture, these programs are not coordinated by any one entity and often overlap. Perhaps one of the unintended challenges for new students resulting from such an array of programs is deciding which ones to participate in. Central coordination could result in a sharper focus, more efficient use of staff time, and a clearer path for students to follow during the first few months.

Conclusion

Kuh, Kinzie, Schuh, Whitt, and Associates (2005) stated clearly the importance of students' out-of-class experiences. The work of student affairs staff must reflect the academic mission in order to assist students in achieving their goals. Student affairs educators often have different forums and locales than faculty do for their teaching. Their responsibilities require that they not only be supervisors, planners, and administrators but also use their skills in ways that educate students through experience and reflection. The focus should not be on developing additional programs that capture students' time and attention for entertainment but rather partnering to enhance their learning experiences both in and out of classrooms.

References

American Association for Higher Education, American College Personnel Association, and National Association of Student Personnel Administrators. *Powerful Partnerships: A Shared Responsibility for Learning.* Washington, D.C.: AAHE, ACPA, and NASPA, 1998.

Astin, A. W. "Student Involvement: A Developmental Theory for Higher Education." *Journal of College Student Development,* 1984, 25(4), 297–308.

Astin, A. W. *What Matters in College? Four Critical Years Revisited.* San Francisco: Jossey-Bass, 1993.

Blimling, G. S., and Alschuler, A. S. "Creating a Home for the Spirit of Learning: Contributions of Student Development Educators." *Journal of College Student Development,* 1996, 37(2), 203–216.

Bloland, P. A., Stamatakos, L. C., and Rogers, R. R. "Redirecting the Role of Student Affairs to Focus on Student Learning." *Journal of College Student Development,* 1996, 37(2), 217–226.

Cohen, D. K., Raudenbush, S., and Ball, D. "Resources, Instruction, and Research." In R. Boruch and F. Mosteller (eds.), *Evidence Matters: Randomized Trials in Education Research.* Washington, D.C.: Brookings Institution Press, 2002.

Iowa State University. "Orientation." 2007a. http://www.admissions.iastate.edu/nsp.php. Accessed Jan. 21, 2007.

Iowa State University. "Community of Color Orientation." 2007b. http://www.dso.iastate.edu/msa/firstyear. Accessed Jan. 21, 2007.

Keeling, R. (ed.). *Learning Reconsidered: A Campus-Wide Focus on the Student Experience.* Washington, D.C.: National Association of Student Personnel Administrators and American College Personnel Association, 2004.

King, P. M. "Student Learning in Higher Education." In S. R. Komives, D. Woodard Jr., and Associates (eds.), *Student Services: A Handbook for the Profession.* San Francisco: Jossey-Bass, 2003.

King, P. M., and Baxter Magolda, M. B. "A Developmental Perspective on Learning." *Journal of College Student Development,* 1996, 37(2), 163–173.

Kuh, G. D., Kinzie, J., Schuh, J. H, Whitt, E. J., and Associates. *Student Success in College: Creating Conditions That Matter.* San Francisco: Jossey-Bass, 2005.

National Resource Center for The First-Year Experience and Students in Transition. "Resource Packet." *First Encounters: Creating Purposeful Strategies to Engage New Students* [Teleconference]. Columbia: University of South Carolina, Apr. 21, 2005.

Pascarella, E. "The Influence of On-Campus Living Versus Commuting to College on Intellectual and Interpersonal Self-Concept." *Journal of College Student Personnel,* 1985, 26(4), 292–299.

Pascarella, E. T., Terenzini, P. T., and Blimling, G. S. "The Impact of Residential Life on Students." In C. Schroeder, P. Mable, and Associates (eds.), *Realizing the Educational Potential of Residence Halls.* San Francisco: Jossey-Bass, 1994.

Terenzini, P. T., Pascarella, E. T, and Blimling, G. S. "Students' Out-of-Class Experiences and Their Influence on Learning and Cognitive Development." *Journal of College Student Development,* 1996, 37(2), 149–162.

Tinto, V. *Leaving College: Rethinking the Causes and Cures of Student Attrition.* (2nd ed.) Chicago: University of Chicago Press, 1993.

MIMI BENJAMIN is assistant to the vice president for student affairs and adjunct lecturer in educational leadership and policy studies at Iowa State University.

KURT EARNEST is coordinator for academic services, Department of Residence, Iowa State University.

DOUG GRUENEWALD is codirector of learning communities and adjunct assistant professor in educational leadership and policy studies at Iowa State University.

GINNY ARTHUR is associate director of residence and adjunct assistant professor in educational leadership and policy studies at Iowa State University.

3

The first-year experience movement opens a window of opportunity for student affairs professionals to extend their educational endeavors into the classroom, thus allowing entrance into segments of campus once reserved exclusively for faculty.

New Frontiers for Student Affairs Professionals: Teaching and the First-Year Experience

Mary Stuart Hunter, Kathleen A. Murray

For many years, faculty attitudes were that if college and university students could not succeed, then they should not be in college in the first place. Over the past twenty-five years, increased attention has been devoted to the challenges students face as they transition into higher education. Student success and retention hang in the balance based on that transition. Colleges and universities, unlike other large and complex organizations and systems, have been somewhat slow to recognize the critical importance of new member assimilation into the cultures of the organization. Large corporations have invested significant resources and time to management training for their newest employees. Likewise, the military has a lengthy and comprehensive program for basic training of its recruits. Higher educators have only more recently seen the need to help beginning college students become acclimated to the culture of their institutions and to collegiate learning in general, because these cultures differ significantly from that of high school. This chapter will discuss key issues in the first college year that are crucial to student success and retention and how they may involve student affairs professionals in traditional teaching settings.

NEW DIRECTIONS FOR STUDENT SERVICES, no. 117, Spring 2007 © Wiley Periodicals, Inc.
Published online in Wiley InterScience (www.interscience.wiley.com) • DOI: 10.1002/ss.230

Understanding Student Retention

Access to college during the first century of United States history was limited. Most colleges admitted the children, mostly sons, of wealthy landowners, and they studied a classical curriculum in preparation for careers in the ministry and education. The Morrill Act in 1862 established many new institutions with broader educational missions, and the enactment of the GI Bill in 1944 further enabled students' access to higher education in significant numbers. For perhaps the first time in the history of American higher education, large numbers of students, with varied needs, enrolled, but for a wide array of reasons many did not complete their degrees.

With the influx of large numbers of students with different levels of preparation and readiness for college, the faculty was called upon to help students with concerns beyond course content. The student affairs profession evolved out of the recognition that factors influencing student growth and development extended beyond the classroom. Today the issues that adversely affect student success and retention are many, and institutions frequently attempt to address a lack of student preparedness and other barriers to success with institutional support services. In addition, new and innovative programs and initiatives have evolved designed to enhance student learning and success for all students, not just for those who need special assistance.

Several theories of student retention that are available to practitioners are supported by research and can serve to support student success. One early theory of student retention identifies factors related to the congruence of student and institutional fit. According to Tinto (1993), a high degree of congruence between the student's values, goals, and attitudes and those of the college increase the likelihood that the student will persist at the college.

Other theories of student retention are related to student involvement and the development of a sense of community (Astin, 1977; Kuh, Kinzie, Schuh, Whitt, and Associates, 2005; Light, 2001). These theories suggest that a direct link exists between the quality and quantity of involvement in activities and students' academic performance and satisfaction. An additional school of thought involves social and academic integration (Tinto, 1993; Pascarella and Terenzini, 2005). When students are able to integrate the in-class and outside-of-class aspects of their lives, they reap great benefits. Recent views on student retention have led to a rethinking of student retention concepts. Braxton (2000) suggests that student persistence is a far more complicated puzzle and involves the four logically interconnected propositions of economic, organizational, psychological, and sociological relationships. Another view is directed at the simple notion of student learning, where learning is identified as the root of student persistence (Astin, 1977; Tinto, 1993; Kuh, Kinzie, Schuh, Whitt, and Associates, 2005; Pascarella and Terenzini, 2005; Light, 2001). Simply put, students who learn are students who stay at an institution, or at the very least, stay engaged in higher education at the same or a different institution.

NEW DIRECTIONS FOR STUDENT SERVICES • DOI: 10.1002/ss

Learning as Key to Student Success and Retention

The publication in 1994 of the American College Personnel Association's *Student Learning Imperative* stimulated discussion and debate on how student affairs professionals can intentionally create the conditions that enhance student learning and personal development. This volume argued that the concepts of learning, personal development, and student development are inextricably intertwined and inseparable and that experiences both in the classroom and in out-of-class settings on and off the campus contribute to learning and personal development. It further suggested that student affairs professionals are indeed educators who share in the responsibility for creating conditions where students are likely to spend time and energy in educationally purposefully activities.

The following year, in 1995, Robert Barr and John Tagg published a landmark article in *Change* entitled "From Teaching to Learning: A New Paradigm for Undergraduate Education." The juxtaposition between teaching and learning is an interesting one. This work encouraged educators to change their view of methods in postsecondary education from one focusing on "instructing students" to one focusing on "creating learning" for students. This new paradigm set "student learning and success" as the boundary (p. 15) and called for colleges to take control of student learning and their learning outcomes.

Barr and Tagg's work was the first of many recent documents encouraging educators to look at student learning as a whole and to do whatever it takes to "produce 'quality learning' and refer to the college's 'learning programs'" (p. 25). The Association of American Colleges and Universities' 2002 report, *Greater Expectations: A New Vision for Learning as a Nation Goes to College,* builds on Barr and Tagg's learning paradigm concept and calls for educators to "promote the kind of learning students need to meet emerging challenges in the workplace, in a diverse democracy, and in an interconnected world" (p. vii). *Greater Expectations* again focuses on the whole student as an intentional learner who is empowered, informed, and responsible and who is, ideally, able to integrate learning from experiences and from formal education in high school and college.

Shortly after *Greater Expectations* was published, the National Association of Student Personnel Administrators and the American College Personnel Association collaborated to create *Learning Reconsidered: A Campus-Wide Focus on the Student Experience* (Keeling, 2004). This document calls for the collaboration of academic affairs and student affairs divisions in producing the whole student. The holistic development of the student should be the primary concern; however, in order to continually address the needs of student learning, the "student affairs divisions must provide ongoing staff development programs designed to introduce new learning in all areas of student affairs practice, to assist staff in the development of new skills, and to ensure that they are fully prepared to meet the new challenges that will face them as we move forward in the twenty-first century" (p. 32).

New Directions for Student Services • DOI: 10.1002/ss

The First-Year Experience Movement

During the same time period that these important documents were published, attention to the student transition to college was gaining significant momentum. Yet attention to student success and retention in the first year of college is not a new phenomenon. In 1877 Johns Hopkins University formed a system of faculty advisors, and Harvard University had a board of freshman advisors as early as 1889 (Gordon, 1989). These recognitions that students come to campus with special needs unique to the first year led to an assortment of programs and organizational strategies to address student needs. Noncredit orientation to college courses were created during the following twenty years at Boston University, the University of Michigan, and Oberlin College; Fitts and Swift noted in 1928 that Reed College offered the first accredited orientation to college course in 1911 (Gordon, 1989).

More recently faculty and staff have worked to improve the transition experience for beginning college students. The modern first-year experience (FYE) movement began in the late 1970s, gained momentum in the 1980s, flourished in the 1990s, and continues today. The creation of the first-year seminar at the University of South Carolina in 1972 by then president Thomas Jones in response to a campus riot is perhaps the most significant event leading to the FYE movement. It was Jones's vision that a course with specially trained instructors would help first-year students transition more successfully to the university environment. The experimental course included an instructor development component that involved student affairs professionals along with faculty. Throughout the 1970s the course at the University of South Carolina underwent sustained assessment, yielding positive and statistically significant results. As John N. Gardner, then director of the course, Charles H. Witten, then chief student affairs officer, and Paul P. Fidler, course assessor, presented sessions at national courses on the University of South Carolina's University 101 program, other institutions sought assistance in replicating the program on their own campuses.

The 1980s saw the interest in first-year seminars gain energy. Campuses of all types were adapting the freshman seminar concept to meet the needs of their campus and students. In 1982, John N. Gardner organized a national conference on the freshman seminar–freshman orientation course concept. Response to the meeting far exceeded expectations and led to a subsequent national conference with a broadened focus. Thus the first of what has become an annual national conference on the freshman year experience was held in 1983. By 1985, educators saw that if the first-year seminar was going to meet its potential on a national level, a literature base and substantial research were needed. This led administrators of the program at the University of South Carolina to seek approval from the South Carolina Commission on Higher Education to establish a national center to serve in a formal capacity the role that it was already serving in a de facto fashion. Thus the National Research Center for The Freshman-Year Experience was founded in 1986 with a mission to encourage research, publish and disseminate research and best practices, and continue to organize continuing education events for higher educators desiring to enhance the first-year experience. By the end of the decade, a semiannual academic research journal and a quarterly newsletter were born, a monograph series was launched, and the annual conference series on the first-year experience continued to grow. These developments enabled many more educators to convince their campus leaders of the efficacy of such programs, thus providing impetus to this growing movement.

The decade of the 1990s was one of exponential growth in the first-year experience movement. The center's publication list grew, the conference series expanded to consider other student transitions beyond the first year, and the name of the center changed twice in response to an expanding mission and the desire to describe itself in a more semantically appropriate manner. Research on issues surrounding the first college year began appearing in a wide range of other journals and periodicals. Conferences of student affairs organizations also frequently included sessions presenting information on institutional initiatives in the first year. But perhaps the technological advances during the 1990s provided the most potent force for growth. Higher education's embrace of Internet technology enabled the center to establish a Web site and several topical listservs, making communication and resource sharing on this important topic much more viable.

In the new millennium, colleges and universities continue to recognize the need to assist students in transition, and the National Resource Center for The First-Year Experience and Students in Transition continues to meet the research and continuing education needs of higher educators. The revised mission statement of the center, "to support and advance efforts to improve student learning and transitions into and through higher education" (National Resource Center for The First-Year Experience and Students in Transition, 2006) reflects its continued work. But the center is not alone in its recognition of the transition to college as a critical one. Philanthropic foundations have also recognized its importance. Such support enabled the creation and development of a number of initiatives positively affecting the first college year, such as the Foundations of Excellence project of the Policy Center on the First Year of College, the National Survey of Student Engagement developed at Indiana University-Bloomington, and the Your First College Year survey at UCLA's Higher Education Research Institute.

Central Elements for Effective Teaching and Working with Students

Early on in the FYE movement, it became evident to many involved in this work that the first year was indeed important. But it became just as apparent that the central issues were about student transitions in a more generic sense than simply about the transition to the first year of college. Several elements central to the first-year experience movement are grounded in student development theory and student retention theory and are foundations of effective teaching and working with students in other capacities.

Understanding Students. Student attitudes, behaviors, and experiences change over time. With each entering class the culture and world affairs that shaped their development were different. Educators need only read the annual Mindset List disseminated by Beloit College (http://www.beloit.edu/~pubaff/mindset/) or the annual release of the Cooperative Institutional Research Program's Freshman Survey results (annual summary of survey findings available at http://www.gseis.ucla.edu/heri/heri.html) to understand that the life experiences students have and the world events that shape them change over time. Faculty and staff must remember that the current undergraduate experience is not necessarily similar to the experience they had as students. Attention to student characteristics, needs, behaviors, and experiences is essential to effective teaching.

Acknowledging Cultural Differences. Another key ingredient in successful teaching is the recognition that beginning college students are moving from one cultural environment to another. Colleges and universities are no different from other complex organizations. Simple osmosis will not transform new students into successful students. The freshman year is not grade thirteen for students. The collegiate culture is very different from the high school culture or the working world culture from which our students come. Deliberate and intentional efforts to help new college students understand the keys to successful learning at the collegiate level are essential if transitional students are to flourish.

Defining Student Success. No quantity of good intentions or hard work by campus faculty and staff will ensure student success if there is no definition of success against which to measure efforts. Measuring success involves quality assessment and program development. Good assessment efforts must begin with the end in mind. Thus, a central element of any program desiring to enable student success must first have a well-developed and articulated definition of success, set of goals, or statement of philosophy. Useful definitions or goal statements of student success should be campus-specific and collaboratively developed. The Orientation and New Student Programs Advisory Committee at the University of Wisconsin-Madison created a set of five first-year student goals. They encourage all members of the UW-Madison community to use the goals as a basis for interactions with first-year students. The five goals are gaining confidence and competence as a college-level student; making positive connections with faculty, staff, and peers; engaging in behaviors that promote personal health and balance; understanding oneself as a member of the socially diverse university community; and developing awareness of the impact of personal choices. Each articulated goal is followed by a list of statements that provide examples of behaviors that indicate the goal has been met.

Preparing for Effective Teaching. Faculty and staff development initiatives are important as well. Traditional graduate preparation programs for student affairs professionals rarely include courses on teaching pedagogy. Understanding student development theory and student personnel services is not enough background for effective teaching. Those who choose to teach and desire to be effective teachers must consider effective pedagogy and learning theories on top of their expertise in student development. The first-year experience movement has had instructor development as a key component from the beginning. Workshops to prepare instructors to teach first-year seminars and other courses in learning communities have been central features. Such training and development programs include a focus on student characteristics and demographics, active learning pedagogies, learning outcomes development, resource development, and evaluation and assessment techniques.

Teaching Opportunities for Student Affairs Professionals

Student affairs professionals now have far more opportunities to engage in classroom teaching than were available in years past. A variety of entry points exist. Many campuses provide such opportunities in first-year seminars, peer educator courses, learning communities, residence halls, academic advising, supplemental instructing, and by forming collaborative relationships between faculty and staff and across departments.

Curriculum Development. Regardless of the type of course taught, student affairs professionals have the opportunity to use their knowledge of student development theory and their vast experience in working with students to inform curriculum development. Knowledge and thorough mastery of course content are certainly prerequisite to successful teaching and learning, but effective pedagogy is of equal importance. Thus, both content and process contribute to student learning in any course setting.

A four-phase model for curriculum development was constructed by the founders of the first-year seminar at the University of South Carolina. The model is easily adaptable to other courses and learning settings. Phase One is a *group building* phase and includes attention to the group of learners where deliberate and educationally purposeful activities are designed to create a congenial group of learners. Icebreakers and other activities are organized to eliminate the anxieties that students bring with them to a new class, to increase communication among students, and to help students get to know one another. Phase Two includes *identification of learner needs and characteristics* in the learning framework. What do students already know about course content and what do they need to learn to be successful in the course? Defining learning outcomes for the course can be collaboratively developed, giving students increased levels of ownership of the course than might exist if their needs and characteristics were not considered. Phase Three follows logically as it focuses on *developing resources to meet learner needs*. Teaching and learning become a collaborative process with students joining the instructor in teaching course content and employing various

New Directions for Student Services • DOI: 10.1002/ss

pedagogies. The final phase is *bridging and transition*. Learning activities include both reflection and projection as students consider all that has been learned in the course and how that knowledge might be used in the future and beyond the parameters of the course. Culminating activities such as final projects, exams, papers, and presentations help students make personal meaning of the course content and appreciate their learning experience.

First-Year Seminars. Student affairs professionals often gain entry to the teaching realm through first-year seminars. Many four-year colleges and universities, and to a somewhat lesser extent, community colleges, offer some form of a first-year seminar. The majority of institutions use professionals with a master's degree or higher as instructors of these seminars. These courses give student affairs professionals the opportunity to interact with students in a classroom setting while also helping them understand the basics of college life, such as managing time, getting involved, study skills, and orienting students to their new educational setting. In this role, student affairs professionals assume an adjunct faculty role by creating a syllabus, grading students' work, and preparing lessons for each class meeting. Teaching a first-year seminar is one of the more common ways for student affairs professionals to gain access to the classroom.

Peer Educator Training Courses. Similar in some ways to first-year seminars are peer educator courses. A growing trend in first-year seminars is to incorporate peer or graduate leaders to coteach with the instructor. Along with coteaching, students may be required to enroll in a supplemental course to assist them through the experience of coteaching a course. In addition to teaching first-year seminars, other peer educators help teach academic courses for students, such as peer health educators, residence hall staff, and diversity program peer educators. Student affairs professionals may have the opportunity to teach these courses, which provide an opportunity to teach upperclassmen. These ever-expanding teaching opportunities for student affairs staff give professionals a chance to work with a different population of students in a different setting.

Learning Communities. Residential and curricular learning communities are a growing entry point for student affairs professionals to get involved in classroom teaching. Learning communities can take a variety of forms, including linked courses, themed courses, and living and learning together as a community. Student affairs professionals are often involved in these initiatives by helping create the link between the faculty and staff. Student affairs professionals understand the importance of campus involvement in the students' college experience. This knowledge can be a driving force to create these communities on individual campuses. Learning communities frequently incorporate service learning projects or other activities that the class participates in as a group. Student affairs professionals can initiate the formation of such communities, facilitate activities, serve as instructors for introductory classes, make connections for residential programs, and administer the learning communities on individual campuses.

NEW DIRECTIONS FOR STUDENT SERVICES • DOI: 10.1002/ss

Some learning communities are solely living and learning communities with no academic courses associated with the program. Student affairs professionals in residence life then become the primary facilitators for these communities and direct the intentional creation of the student learning experiences. Although this is not a classroom setting, the learning that occurs outside of the classroom is as important as any traditional learning opportunity. Residential staffs create these learning experiences in learning communities and direct the programming that exists in the residence halls as well. A number of initiatives, such as academic tutoring centers, academic advising, and educational and motivational speakers, often present to residence hall staffs and the students living in the hall as well. Increasingly, residence halls are creating space for classrooms inside the building in order to bring the learning directly to where the students spend the majority of their time. This helps students more effortlessly make the cognitive connection between living on campus and learning.

Peer-Assisted Study. An academic initiative that can be administered either in student affairs or in academic affairs, Supplemental Instruction (SI) is a validated initiative that targets traditionally difficult introductory classes—those with high failure and withdrawal rates. Student affairs professionals involved with these programs have the opportunity to teach students how to teach their peers. They learn to understand different learning styles and different pedagogies. When administered through student affairs, SI creates the need for professionals to understand teaching and learning and helps student leaders implement good, additional instruction for the courses.

Team Teaching. Student affairs professionals often have the opportunity to become involved in classroom teaching in a team-teaching format with faculty. Team teaching frequently yields better student learning, regardless of the team composition. But learning is not limited to the students in the class. The benefit of such team-teaching arrangements is reciprocal. Student affairs staff can help faculty better understand student development issues, and faculty can help student affairs staff learn teaching techniques and pedagogy.

Concluding Thoughts

Student affairs professionals have much to offer students and coteachers in the classroom. In order for student affairs professionals to become involved in classroom teaching, most entry points require a collaborative effort between the faculty and staff, or more specifically, between student affairs and academic affairs. Support from campus leaders is essential for efforts to find success. Both student affairs and academic affairs divisions must be willing to work toward the initiatives that will facilitate student learning and not rely on "what has been done in the past." Successful implementation of new and exciting programs is more likely when there is input from both faculty and staff. Faculty members understand the intricacies of teaching and have the content knowledge required for specific courses or disciplines, and student affairs staff members understand student growth and development.

NEW DIRECTIONS FOR STUDENT SERVICES • DOI: 10.1002/ss

Student affairs professionals can focus on their strengths and knowledge of student development to enhance student success, involvement, and retention. With the growing number of teaching opportunities available during first-year experience initiatives, student affairs professionals can have a great influence on first-year students' relationship with their institution and with student learning. Optimal student learning takes place when all elements are present.

References

American College Personnel Association. *The Student Learning Imperative: Implications for Student Affairs.* Washington, D.C.: American College Personnel Association, 1994.

Association of American Colleges and Universities. *Greater Expectations: A New Vision for Learning as a Nation Goes to College.* Washington, D.C.: Association of American Colleges and Universities, 2002.

Astin, A. W. *Four Critical Years.* San Francisco: Jossey-Bass, 1977.

Barr, R. B., and Tagg, J. "From Teaching to Learning: A New Paradigm for Undergraduate Education." *Change,* Nov.-Dec. 1995, pp. 12–25.

Braxton, J. M. (ed.). *Reworking the Student Departure Puzzle.* Nashville: Vanderbilt University Press, 2000.

Gordon, V. N. "Origins and Purposes of the Freshman Seminar." In M. L. Upcraft, J. N. Gardner, and Associates (eds.), *The Freshman Year Experience: Helping Students Survive and Succeed in College.* San Francisco: Jossey-Bass, 1989.

Keeling, R. (ed.). *Learning Reconsidered: A Campus-Wide Focus on the Student Experience.* Washington, D.C.: National Association of Student Personnel Administrators and American College Personnel Association, 2004.

Kuh, G. D., Kinzie, J., Schuh, J. H., Whitt, E. J., and Associates. *Student Success in College: Creating Conditions That Matter.* San Francisco: Jossey-Bass, 2005.

Light, R. J. *Making the Most of College: Students Speak Their Minds.* Boston: Harvard University Press, 2001.

National Resource Center for The First-Year Experience and Students in Transition. 2006. http://www.sc.edu/fye. Accessed May 24, 2006.

Pascarella, E. T., and Terenzini, P. T. *How College Affects Students.* Vol. 2. San Francisco: Jossey-Bass, 2005.

Tinto, V. *Leaving College: Rethinking the Causes and Cures of Student Attrition.* (2nd ed.) Chicago: University of Chicago Press, 1993.

MARY STUART HUNTER is director of the National Resource Center for The First-Year Experience and Students in Transition at the University of South Carolina, where she has taught the first-year seminar for twenty-eight years. In addition to her administrative work with the center, she cofacilitates the faculty development workshops required for all first-year seminar instructors.

KATHLEEN A. MURRAY is the first-year mentor at Goucher College. She is a recent graduate of the Higher Education and Student Affairs program at the University of South Carolina, where she was a graduate assistant at the National Resource Center for The First-Year Experience and Students in Transition. During her graduate studies she served as a graduate leader and coteacher for the first-year seminar.

4

In this chapter, the authors consider various teaching roles that student affairs professionals may fulfill in learning communities, as well as the potential professional development that results from involvement.

Reframing Teaching and Learning: Lessons from Learning Communities for Student Affairs

Shari Ellertson, Karla V. Thoennes

It is well-known in the student affairs profession that practitioners in student affairs are facilitators of student development (American College Personnel Association, 1994; Evans, Forney, and Guido-DiBrito, 1998). However, do student affairs professionals also view themselves as teachers, or are they more likely to associate that role with faculty and in-class activities? In this chapter, we will explore student affairs professionals' roles as teachers and learners in learning communities. Learning communities are one example of how academic and student affairs can collaborate in a joint effort to facilitate student learning and development. Learning communities, we believe, are one venue in which student affairs professionals can explicitly demonstrate their roles as facilitators of student learning and partners in the educational process—that is, as teachers.

We begin this chapter with a brief review of how learning communities fit with student affairs' goals and philosophies of teaching and learning. We then explore the lessons that can be gleaned from learning communities about reframing teaching and learning and how this reframing can benefit student affairs. Next, we discuss learning community models and the various roles that student affairs professionals can fulfill in them. In our next section, we present ideas about how student affairs professionals can themselves gain professional development through involvement with learning communities. Finally, we conclude with challenges and opportunities for student

NEW DIRECTIONS FOR STUDENT SERVICES, no. 117, Spring 2007 © Wiley Periodicals, Inc.
Published online in Wiley InterScience (www.interscience.wiley.com) • DOI: 10.1002/ss.231

affairs professionals working with learning communities, as well as our hopes for future expansion of the teaching roles that student affairs professionals can fulfill in learning communities. In addition, we share our experiences, insights, and some ponderings that may be useful to others who are exploring ways in which student affairs professionals are teachers and facilitators of student learning and development.

A Part, Not Apart: Learning Communities, Collaborative Efforts, and Shared Aims

Over the past decade, learning communities have emerged as an example of institutional response to calls for national reform in higher education. The Wingspread Group (1993), the Boyer Commission (1998), and the Association of American Colleges and Universities (2002) all called for the refocusing of education on student learning.

The pedagogy of learning communities provides a unique opportunity for student affairs and academic affairs to collaborate around the goal of connected (or integrative) learning. The value of collaborations between student affairs and academic affairs has been affirmed in documents such as *Powerful Partnerships* (American Association for Higher Education, American College Personnel Association, and National Association of Student Personnel Administrators, 1998) and *Principles of Good Practice for Student Affairs* (American College Personnel Association and National Association of Student Personnel Administrators, 1997), which complement the existing desires of student affairs professionals to be active participants in helping students bridge in- and out-of-class learning. In addition, the *Student Learning Imperative* (American College Personnel Association, 1994) explicitly encourages student affairs professionals to collaborate with others to promote student learning and development.

The roots of the modern-day learning community can be traced back to the work of Alexander Meiklejohn and John Dewey (Gabelnick, MacGregor, Matthews, and Smith, 1990). Meiklejohn is considered a father of learning community work, with his Experimental College at the University of Wisconsin taking shape in the 1920s. Meiklejohn's approach was revolutionary in that he reorganized the structure of the curriculum in order to provide an integrated education where topics were not studied in isolation, thus contributing to modern-day learning communities through the creation of alternative curricular structures. His legacy fits with a contemporary definition of learning communities as "a variety of curricular approaches that intentionally link or cluster two or more courses, often around an interdisciplinary theme or problem, and enroll a common cohort of students" (Smith, MacGregor, Matthews, and Gabelnick, 2004, p. 20). Learning communities, therefore, push the boundaries of education by rethinking the traditional curriculum and attempting to integrate and make cohesive the learning experience, just as student affairs professionals attempt to provide a "seamless" environment for learning.

Dewey, on the other hand, made contributions to modern-day learning communities through his philosophy of education (Gabelnick, MacGregor, Matthews, and Smith, 1990). His views on education are aligned with a constructivist epistemology—that is, according to Dewey "education is seen as a more open-ended inquiry process rather than a teacher-dominated process of 'handing down' knowledge as a finished product" (p. 16). Dewey promoted close relationships between students and teachers and advocated for more coherent (and less fragmented) learning. His philosophy mirrors the goals of the student affairs practitioner—that is, to focus holistically on students and develop relationships that allow "teachable moments" to emerge.

Thus, learning communities and student affairs complement rather than compete with each other in their aims to focus holistically on students, integrate the student learning experience, and engage directly with students.

Learning Community Models

By 2003, learning communities were implemented in various forms at over six hundred colleges and universities in the United States (The Evergreen State College, 2004). Examples of learning community models include coordinated studies, federated learning communities, linked or clustered courses, freshman interest groups (FIGs), living-learning communities, gateway courses, and general education (Matthews, Smith, MacGregor, and Gabelnick, 1996; Smith, MacGregor, Matthews, and Gabelnick, 2004). In general, the differences in these models have to do with the structure of the curriculum, faculty roles, the use of seminars, and types of community-building activities (Gabelnick, MacGregor, Matthews, and Smith, 1990). However, there are no clear-cut definitions of what a learning community comprises; institution-specific models have emerged as individual institutions have implemented their own versions of learning communities, sometimes by adapting or modifying various models.

Regardless of the model, student affairs professionals can fulfill a variety of teaching roles, although perhaps most notably in living-learning programs or other learning community models that have been built into existing campus programs, such as the first-year experience (FYE).

Student Affairs Teaching Roles in Learning Communities

Aside from involvement in learning community programs, student affairs professionals already serve in a multitude of teaching roles, both formal and informal. For example, formal teaching roles may include teaching leadership workshops, creating educational programming in the residence halls, or training student staff members. Informal teaching occurs in many forms, such as in one-on-one discussions with students, advising a student organization, or serving as a role model. Student affairs professionals often refer to these as "teachable moments," meaning that one is never quite certain when the opportunity to influence student learning and growth may occur. All of these formal and informal teaching experiences can enhance what student affairs professionals contribute to learning communities. However, learning communities also can provide new ways for student affairs staff to execute their teaching roles, both in and out of the classroom.

As learning communities challenge traditional boundaries of education, student affairs and academic affairs can challenge the perceived boundaries in the academy by sharing, communicating, and expanding their roles. Student affairs staff can take on roles as instructors of learning community courses or seminars, such as first-year experience or orientation courses that may be linked with one or more courses in the learning community. Often, the first-year experience–orientation course or seminar serves both as an introduction to campus life and an introduction to the student's major. Thus, these courses can be catalysts for collaborations between student affairs and academic affairs, in which academic affairs can share in the student development aspects of the students' orientation to campus while student affairs can share in acclimating students to a disciplinary program. Another unique possibility afforded through this approach is the opportunity to team-teach the course with a faculty member. This fosters even closer connections between the work of academic and student affairs. As previously mentioned, learning communities push the boundaries of the traditional roles of teacher and student; thus, student affairs staff also benefit as learners, a topic we will discuss at more length later in this chapter.

Residence-based learning communities provide opportunities for residence life professionals and paraprofessionals to fulfill direct and indirect teaching roles with learning community participants. For example, hall directors at North Dakota State University provide venues, activities, and support for students in learning communities as they form relationships with their cohorts in the residence hall. The bonds created among the students help create an environment both in and out of the classroom where discussion and engagement come more naturally and enhance the learning experience. Students may use and practice the problem-based learning techniques they are developing in the classroom through leadership roles in the residence hall, through hall governments, or through other residence life opportunities in which hall directors play a role.

Further, residence hall staff and other student affairs professionals can play a significant role in putting the "community" into the learning community. A highly successful learning community goes beyond enhancing students' familiarity and comfort with one another. A true learning community exists when students are able to recognize that their role in the community goes beyond what they will gain personally. They will know, understand, and be invested in the goals of the entire community; be invested in learning outcomes for themselves and their cohorts; and be able to recognize that how they perform and act in the community has an impact on how the community will succeed. Student affairs professionals know that simply having a pizza party will not create a community; instead, the community has to be intentionally nurtured. Student affairs professionals are well-versed in teaching students about how to build such a community and play a significant educational role in helping create it.

Some learning community programs also employ peer mentors, who are hired specifically to enrich the learning community experience for student participants. Learning community mentors at North Dakota State University are charged with developing one-on-one relationships with students in their cohort, with the mentors assisting students in both personal and academic learning and development. These mentors also facilitate leadership workshops for learning community participants on topics such as personality profiles, developing integrity, and leadership styles. Iowa State University has developed a strong model for learning community peer mentors in which the mentors serve in a variety of roles, from coteaching courses, to facilitating group study sessions, to meeting with students individually on academic or personal issues. In these ways, the peer mentors serve in both formal and informal teaching roles (for more information, see Benjamin, Chrystal, Earnest, and Grube, 2005).

A myriad of other student affairs professionals can contribute to the development and success of a learning community. These individuals can take on both formal and informal teaching roles as well. For example, academic success professionals can provide teaching through educational sessions and workshops presented to learning community students on topics such as study skills, time management, and test taking. They also may serve as teachers of peer mentors; for instance, at North Dakota State University, training for the mentors included a session on learning styles facilitated by professionals from the Orientation and Student Success Office. Academic success professionals also may coordinate the roles of student paraprofessionals as the Academic Success Center does with Supplemental Instruction (SI) leaders at Iowa State University. The SI leaders also fulfill a teaching role in learning communities by facilitating study sessions.

Student affairs colleagues in areas other than academic success may also play a teaching role with learning community participants and mentors. For instance, financial aid professionals may present a session for students on debt management or budgeting, counseling center staff may present a session on assertiveness skills or conflict resolution, and student activities professionals may facilitate a session on leadership styles. Mentor training may include sessions from the registrar's office on academic advising or a workshop on student development from the Dean of Students Office. In each of these examples, the goal is to enhance the learning community experience.

NEW DIRECTIONS FOR STUDENT SERVICES • DOI: 10.1002/ss

Of course, any programmatic strategies used with the learning community should complement the overall goals of the program and contribute to the intended learning outcomes for participants. In other words, programs need to be carefully selected as part of the overall design of the learning community. Being part of the design phase of a learning community is another way student affairs professionals can contribute to student learning. Specific offices such as multicultural affairs, TRIO programs, student activities, and others may be involved with learning community design or coordination of learning communities for the student populations with whom they work or around a particular topic of expertise (such as leadership).

Overall, there are many ways in which student affairs professionals and paraprofessionals serve as teachers in learning communities. As we work to challenge and extend our roles through learning communities, we may reap the rewards of participation by enhancing our own professional development, which is the focus of the next section.

Professional Development: Becoming Better Teachers Through Learning Community Involvement

Levine Laufgraben and Shapiro (2004) discuss faculty development as one of the critical factors in sustaining and improving learning communities. This too must be the focus for student affairs professionals working with learning communities. Student affairs professionals are provided the opportunity to grow and develop professionally in ways that may be different from those we have traditionally experienced in professional development. Working with a learning community affords "on-the-job" training that can expand skills and knowledge and can then be applied to other of our teaching roles.

Walking a Mile in Their Shoes. Most learning communities involve student affairs professionals working with faculty, administrators, and students in planning, implementation, and evaluation. This unique institutional collaboration parallels some of the very experiences students face when beginning their college career. Students are becoming acclimated to a new cultural context and facing the risks of new situations.

Cultural Context. Just as a new college student often is stepping into a brand new culture, the same could be said for the team of individuals working to develop a learning community program. A successful learning community will involve individuals from multiple areas in the institution. These may include faculty members, residence life, registrar's office, orientation, academic advisors, faculty members, assessment and research coordinators, and many others. Each stakeholder will come to the table with a different perspective and needs. Each person will see his or her role in the institution and on the team differently. All may also hold differing perspectives about students, in general, and what our individual and collective roles with students should be. Finally, they may have very different ideas and theories about teaching and learning.

NEW DIRECTIONS FOR STUDENT SERVICES • DOI: 10.1002/ss

In addition, members of the learning community team also will have differing ways of seeing and performing their work. Some may desire more meetings, whereas others will avoid them at all costs. Some may be more relationship- and team-oriented, whereas others would rather focus on tasks and individual responsibilities. Schedules and workloads also may be seen differently, and the compensation and reward structures may vary greatly for each member of the team. These variations in work life alone can create their own set of challenges.

Working on a learning community project challenges members to stretch themselves to gain new perspectives and think about new ways of doing their work. In a sense, the learning community team must create its own culture, one in which all members can be fulfilled and successful. College students not only come away with an end product—their degree—but also come away with a new way of seeing the world, a new cultural context, which will help them be more successful professionals and citizens. So too will student affairs professionals come away not only with the end product of a learning community but also with more ideas about their work and their roles as educators.

Shared Responsibility, Risk Taking, and Humility. Working in a new cultural context also can pose challenges as student affairs professionals negotiate their roles and determine how they will best contribute to the learning community program. It is important for them to demonstrate their importance to the project as they listen and learn from others. For example, student affairs professionals can contribute knowledge of and experience with student development theory and practice in the integration of the learning community concept. In this way, they can help educate other members of the team who do not have this knowledge and experience. This "teaching" role can include sharing literature, data, or other resources that stem from the extensive knowledge base on higher education, including topics such as college students and their development, retention issues, and higher education policy, to name a few. Although engaging in this kind of teaching (of faculty and other members of the team) can come with some risk and require some humility, it can bring great rewards in terms of new relationships, mutual understanding, and ultimately, learning for our students.

To effectively bring our voice to the table, student affairs professionals must carefully draw from our knowledge base and put ourselves "out front" on the issues while at the same time recognizing that faculty also have knowledge and skills in this area based on their experiences with students. It is true that we are in touch with students' opinions, feelings, and needs. It is true that we care about the student as a whole person (intellectually, physically, spiritually, emotionally, and so on). It is true that we know and understand student development and can apply theory to our daily practice. It is true that we are innovators and promoters of change. It is true that we are dedicated teachers, always looking for the teachable moment. It is true that we are capable and intelligent scholars. But so are faculty. Just as we provide a balance for academic affairs, they provide a balance for us. This is where our humility is of great importance. We must be willing to share the responsibility for student success, and shared responsibility requires an acknowledgment that we do not have the corner on student development, just as academic affairs faculty do not have the corner on student learning. It is only when we open up our traditional boundaries that we can open ourselves to new learning, the opportunities for which are abundant in the learning community.

Even if the approach is different, both student affairs professionals and faculty have perspectives about students that will contribute to the discussion about learning communities. Depending on the culture that has been created by the learning community team, the level of risk taking and humility required will vary. In essence, however, it is important to seek to create a collaborative environment, honoring the contributions of all members of the team.

Expanding Knowledge and Skills. Working in a learning community offers student affairs professionals the opportunity and the challenge to expand our knowledge. First, to be fully integrated into the project we must have knowledge about the different areas of the institution contributing to the learning community. These may include residence life, admissions, orientation, registration, academic advising, student academic services, and service learning. Further, gaining knowledge about the requirements for general education and degree programs would be helpful for seeing the big picture of the project. Increasing knowledge about various technology-based learning tools, such as Blackboard or WebCT, online libraries, research engines, and Web technology also will be an important way for student affairs professionals to expand our knowledge, thus improving our roles as teachers.

Skill development is another way learning communities increase the success of student affairs professionals as teachers in these programs. Learning communities should have some element of assessment and research as part of the program. Student affairs professionals engaged in learning communities should develop their skills in assessment and research methods, data interpretation, and utilization of the findings to improve practice (that is, looping). These skills will serve them well not only in the context of the learning community but in all aspects of their professional work.

Understanding curriculum development and honing skills related to teaching methods and pedagogy will not only contribute to the success of the learning community but also will assist student affairs professionals in other teaching roles. Some topical areas to consider include using different teaching methods for various learning styles, problem-based learning, case studies, and experiential learning. In learning communities, the curricula are often designed in ways that overlap the in- and out-of-class experiences. Therefore, developing curriculum for out-of-class activities where student affairs may play the predominant role is imperative. The out-of-class experiences in a learning community should complement the overall goals of the program and should be intentionally designed, including targeting specific

NEW DIRECTIONS FOR STUDENT SERVICES • DOI: 10.1002/ss

learning outcomes and using appropriate assessment strategies. Another aspect of designing a learning community cocurriculum is to consider how academic and professional skills, such as problem solving, decision making, knowledge application, and teamwork, can be fostered through out-of-class activities. In cases where student affairs professionals are involved in a disciplinary-based learning community, there is a further opportunity to learn discipline-specific research on curriculum development and teaching and learning as well as to expand one's knowledge of the discipline itself.

Finally, developing a successful learning community requires programmatic sustainability, financially and through faculty, staff, and student participation. Student affairs professionals, therefore, should look to develop their skills in seeking financial resources and marketing. Financial support for learning communities may come from various sources, including internal funds as well as external funds, such as grants and contributions. Marketing the program may include participation in new student events, brochure development, market research, and student-based promotions. Ensuring sustainability through faculty, staff, and student involvement also is crucial, so student affairs professionals should seek to involve others and bring new voices and experiences to the table. Sharing the opportunity with other professionals contributes to the short-term success of the program by bringing in new ideas and long-term success of the program by ensuring that there are committed people to carry on the work.

Making It Work. The simple fact that one is involved in a learning community program can enhance the teaching ability of all members of the team. In the academic affairs area, learning communities often are looked on not only as programs to assist students in being more successful but also as a means for faculty development. The same goal should hold true for the student affairs professionals working with learning communities. Intentional efforts, therefore, should be made to assist student affairs professionals in their development. Some of these efforts may be in collaboration with the faculty development efforts already being offered, such as developmental workshops, team retreats, and teaching-focused conferences and institutes. Since 1999, Iowa State University has sponsored a very successful on-campus Learning Communities Institute. The institute brings together faculty and staff from across campus who work with learning communities in a unique joint professional development opportunity. While providing educational programs and learning opportunities for participants, the institute serves as a catalyst for connecting student affairs professionals, faculty, and administrators. Beyond organized campus events, student affairs professionals may engage in social activities with faculty, visit classrooms, and become familiar with academic affairs–focused books and journals.

Many resources are available as well to help further develop our teaching skills in learning communities. These may require us to step out of our traditional professional development activities and seek new opportunities.

NEW DIRECTIONS FOR STUDENT SERVICES • DOI: 10.1002/ss

For example, the Learning Community National Learning Commons Web site (http://www.evergreen.edu/washcenter), which is sponsored through the Washington Center for Improving the Quality of Undergraduate Education, has a wealth of information that can contribute to our professional development. The Web site contains not only descriptions of learning community programs but articles, papers, and even videos. Thus, professional development is available literally at our fingertips and can happen at our own computer and on our own time. Other national and regional associations often sponsor conferences or meetings that may relate to learning community work. Such organizations include the Association of American Colleges and Universities, various regional learning community networks (accessible from the Learning Community Commons Web site), regional associations such as the Collaboration for the Advancement of College Teaching and Learning, and the Professional and Organizational Development (POD) Network in Higher Education, a group that consists of faculty developers from across the country who are focused on the improvement of teaching and learning in higher education and other organizations. Last, student affairs professionals should consider opportunities to attend disciplinary conferences that focus on teaching and learning together with our faculty collaborators. And we should invite faculty to attend conferences sponsored by our professional associations. We have much to learn from each other, and conferences are one way to expand our levels of understanding and nurture our relationships. Overall, student affairs professionals should seek new and different professional development opportunities to expand our horizons and continue to challenge us to improve as teachers and learners.

New Challenges and Opportunities

As learning communities continue to expand and approaches to implementing them multiply, exciting opportunities are on the horizon for student affairs. We see continued opportunities to develop innovative approaches to our work, both in and out of the classroom, by developing new strategies for integrating the curriculum and cocurriculum. At the same time, opportunities to build bridges with faculty, administrators, and other academic and student affairs colleagues are abundant and should not be overlooked. By engaging in such collaborations, student affairs may influence the development of a new kind of practice and scholarship in higher education. Integrated, collaborative efforts do not simply benefit student and academic affairs positively; ultimately, students are the recipients of richer and deeper learning experiences, which answer the calls for reform in higher education.

Preparing for the future of learning communities also will require student affairs to give attention to how we prepare new professionals for learning community roles. Involving incoming student affairs colleagues is essential for sustaining student affairs' role in learning communities. Preparation programs, in particular, would be an excellent place to acclimate our future colleagues by modeling collaborative, integrative learning; providing teaching internships-projects, practicum experiences, and assistantships; and developing knowledge and skills on curriculum development, pedagogy, and assessment. However, the responsibility does not rest solely with faculty in preparation programs. All of these things can be fostered as well by providers of assistantships, internships, and supervisors of new professionals.

In conclusion, we share our hope that student affairs professionals will embrace the exciting changes in the learning paradigm and expand our roles as both teachers and learners, not only in learning communities but in every facet of what we do. In recognizing our roles as both teachers and learners, we will continue to improve as professionals and make a difference in the lives of our students.

References

American Association for Higher Education, American College Personnel Association, and National Association of Student Personnel Administrators. *Powerful Partnerships: A Shared Responsibility for Learning.* Washington, D.C.: AAHE, ACPA, and NASPA, 1998. http://www.aahe.org/teaching/tsk_frce.htm. Accessed Dec. 18, 2003.

American College Personnel Association. *The Student Learning Imperative: Implications for Student Affairs.* Washington, D.C.: ACPA, 1994. http://www.acpa.nche.edu/sli/sli.htm. Accessed Oct. 4, 2005.

American College Personnel Association and National Association of Student Personnel Administrators. *Principles of Good Practice for Student Affairs: Statement and Inventories.* Washington, D.C.: ACPA and NASPA, 1997.

Association of American Colleges and Universities. *Greater Expectations: A New Vision for Learning as a Nation Goes to College.* Washington, D.C.: AACU, 2002. http://www.greaterexpectations.org. Accessed Oct. 29, 2002.

Benjamin, M., Chrystal, L. L., Earnest, K., and Grube, S. "Peer Mentors in Teaching Roles." 2005. http://www.lc.iastate.edu/PMresearch.html. Accessed Oct. 10, 2005.

Boyer Commission on Educating Undergraduates in the Research University. *Reinventing Undergraduate Education: A Blueprint for America's Research Universities.* 1998. http://naples.cc.sunysb.edu/Pres/boyer.nsf. Accessed Nov. 26, 2002.

Evans, N. J., Forney, D. S., and Guido-DiBrito, F. *Student Development in College: Theory, Research, and Practice.* San Francisco: Jossey-Bass, 1998.

The Evergreen State College. *Learning Communities: Constancy and Change* [Motion picture]. Olympia: Washington Center for Improving the Quality of Undergraduate Education, The Evergreen State College, 2004.

Gabelnick, F., MacGregor, J., Matthews, R. S., and Smith, B. L. *Learning Communities: Creating Connections Among Students, Faculty, and Disciplines.* San Francisco: Jossey-Bass, 1990.

Levine Laufgraben, J., and Shapiro, N. S. *Sustaining and Improving Learning Communities.* San Francisco: Jossey-Bass, 2004.

Matthews, R. S., Smith, B. L., MacGregor, J., and Gabelnick, F. "Creating Learning Communities." In J. G. Gaff, J. L. Ratcliff, and Associates (eds.), *Handbook of the Undergraduate Curriculum: A Comprehensive Guide to Purposes, Structures, Practices, and Change.* San Francisco: Jossey-Bass, 1996.

Smith, B. L., MacGregor, J., Matthews, R. S., and Gabelnick, F. *Learning Communities: Reforming Undergraduate Education.* San Francisco: Jossey-Bass, 2004.

Wingspread Group on Higher Education. *An American Imperative: Higher Expectations for Higher Education.* 1993. http://www.johnsonfdn.org/library/foundpub/amerimp/. Accessed Dec. 17, 2002.

SHARI ELLERTSON *formerly worked with the learning communities program at Iowa State University and currently serves as visiting assistant professor and assessment consultant for the Web and Digital Media Program at the University of Wisconsin-Stevens Point.*

KARLA V. THOENNES *is the associate director of residence life at North Dakota State University. She has worked with a campuswide team to develop and implement the Caring Community of Leaders and Problem Solvers (CCLP) learning communities at North Dakota State University.*

NEW DIRECTIONS FOR STUDENT SERVICES • DOI: 10.1002/ss

Unique opportunities exist on small campuses for all professionals to interact without boundaries. The traditional boundaries of classroom learning and student life cease to exist; student life professionals often function as teachers, and academic affairs professionals are encouraged to support students outside the classroom. This partnership creates many student-focused learning situations that blur the lines between student affairs and academic affairs.

The Many Hats of Teaching in Small Colleges: The Seamless Web of Student and Academic Affairs

Greta Degen, Erin Sheldahl

In the final course of my master's program in higher education student services, a panel of seasoned faculty members sat before my classmates to share their perspectives on the role student development professionals play in student learning. The anticipated chasm between academic affairs and student affairs was evident, as was the dismay and frustration of my student development colleagues. When asked about collaboration between academic affairs and student affairs, one professor noted that while all professionals care about the success of the student, it is as if student affairs exists in a different country, speaking a foreign language. As I reflected on this, I recognized that student development educators must be intentional in their quest to become bilingual in the college culture. This diversification in point of view will perhaps lessen the frustration experienced on both sides of a partnership. Ideally, it will further legitimize the important role student development professionals play as educators, in and out of the classroom. Perhaps more importantly, a willingness to "cross the border" will lessen an evident gap that exists on so many campuses, ultimately facilitating a holistic approach to student learning, growth, and success. [E. Sheldahl, personal communication, 2005]

I recently completed the first class in my doctoral studies at a large university. While participating, I noticed that the differences between my classmates

New Directions for Student Services, no. 117, Spring 2007 © Wiley Periodicals, Inc.
Published online in Wiley InterScience (www.interscience.wiley.com) • DOI: 10.1002/ss.232

and myself were overpowering, inhibiting open discussion between us. All of my classmates were from student affairs; I was from academic affairs. The differences seemed more evident because only a few of my classmates came from a small private college setting such as I did. I was told that it was rare to have faculty address issues surrounding student affairs or to even want to talk about them. As I reflected on this phenomenon, I compared it to my own work setting. It seems that I have unintentionally "crossed the border" between academic and student affairs purely by nature of working in a small campus culture that supports and promotes such interaction. I believe that this is less my own initiative than a necessary adaptation to the work environment of a small, private college. In fact, my coauthor and I work at the same campus, she in student affairs and I in academic affairs. This led us to many interesting and ongoing conversations about partnerships in a small college and to coauthoring this article. [G. Degen, personal communication, 2005]

More opportunities for partnerships between student and academic affairs seem to exist on smaller campuses. One reason could be that there is simply less physical distance between students' living and learning facilities on a small campus compared to larger institutions. Physical distance on a campus can easily lead to communication and service division among its employees serving these purposes. Another reason could be the small campus's focus on student retention as the primary source of funding, compared to competition on larger campuses for outside funding. We believe that smaller campuses are in the best position to support increased collegiality between student affairs and academic affairs professionals. In this chapter, we seek to point out and discuss opportunities and challenges surrounding such existing partnerships on a small Midwestern campus.

Partnerships Between Academic Affairs and Student Affairs: A Review of the Literature

A review of the literature reveals a current trend toward forging relationships between academic affairs and student affairs on college campuses. Recent literature on this topic is based on the DEEP (Documenting Effective Educational Practices) studies supported by the National Survey of Student Engagement and the American Association for Higher Education (Kinzie and Kuh, 2004). Twenty institutions around the country were studied to examine their success that led to higher-than-predicted student engagement and graduation rates. The distinctive campus practices in the DEEP institutions included "collaboration among all parts of the institution" (p. 4), and the strong relationship between student and academic affairs was found to be a major factor in these campuses' success.

There is a definite lack of research connecting small campus environment to successful partnerships between student and academic affairs

NEW DIRECTIONS FOR STUDENT SERVICES • DOI: 10.1002/ss

directly. Functional partnerships described in the literature revolve around specific projects. "Service learning programs are based on partnerships between academic affairs and students affairs" (Jacoby, 1999, p. 19). Cross-campus partnerships, such as freshman interest groups (Schroeder, Minor, and Tarkow, 1999; Westfall, 1999) and assessment of student learning (Kuh and Banta, 2000) were also the trigger for faculty and student affairs to work together to create new opportunities for students.

Much can be learned about existing collaborative efforts on small campuses by reflecting on literature about relationships. Kantor and Lehr (1975) formulated the theory of *structural dynamics*—that is, problems that manifest themselves in relationships are the result of invisible structures—from a study of family interactions. A small campus has fewer invisible structures dividing student and academic affairs and is in a better position to create meaningful relationships between the two. Organizational theorists such as Senge (1994) have theorized about the effects of relationships within teams in an organization. Senge developed the concept of systems thinking in organizations. "There is less leverage in approaching behavior and relationships through individual therapy, and more leverage in studying the team as a system" (p. 408). A smaller campus can offer student and academic affairs the structure and team motivation to partner together successfully.

Magolda (2005) reflected on the relationships between student and academic affairs in DEEP campus cultures. He stated that collaborative efforts between faculty and staff included the common assumption by student affairs professionals that they would take a deferential role. "Too often student affairs professionals have undervalued themselves as experts, despite experiences that might qualify them" (p. 19). Partnerships, therefore, between faculty and staff professionals can often lead to repressed conflict, resulting in a failed collaboration. Magolda urged both student affairs and academic affairs professionals to embrace their conflict by negotiating meaning and celebrating differences early in collaborative efforts. He also suggested that successful collaborative efforts should begin with academic affairs and must include opportunities for both student and academic affairs professionals to discuss their discomforts and differences.

Collaborative partnerships between student and academic affairs professionals on small campuses revolve around finding the best way to engage students in learning. Schuh (1999) discussed principles that guide campus cultures when effective partnerships are present. Emphasis in such successful efforts center around student learning, both in and outside of classrooms. Both staff and faculty must reach out past the usual boundaries of their work environments. This might include staff coteaching with faculty, or faculty interacting with students outside the classroom. Both student and academic affairs professionals must also be involved equally in the political aspects of campus committee work and task forces.

NEW DIRECTIONS FOR STUDENT SERVICES • DOI: 10.1002/ss

The Community of Grand View College

Grand View College (GVC) is a moderately selective undergraduate liberal arts college, affiliated with the Evangelical Lutheran Church of America (ELCA). GVC's current enrollment is approximately 1,750 full-time and part-time students. Located in urban Des Moines, Iowa, GVC has enjoyed healthy enrollment gains throughout recent years. A large percentage of the student body is made up of first-generation college students, many from diverse socioeconomic backgrounds. A majority of those enrolled commute to campus from the surrounding area. The recent award of a five-year Title III grant has allowed GVC to deepen the focus on student success and retention. Efforts have primarily focused on first-year retention in a learning communities model. As the grant years progress, so does the discussion of services and support to all students on campus.

Boundaries. Grand View College is small; the campus is spread the length of one street, or three long blocks. The physical environment presents simple challenges to the wider exchange of ideas between student and academic affairs professionals due to the central location of student affairs in one main building. In our experience, academics walking across campus, for instance, are less apt to encounter student affairs professionals for conversation and more likely to meet other academics. Sparing attempts have been made to physically place student affairs professionals in academic divisions. In the philosophy and religion department, the campus ministers can be found down the hallway from the professors of philosophy and religion and downstairs from residence hall rooms. This intermingling seems to be popular with faculty, staff, and students.

Teaching assignments are not as integrative for student affairs professionals. Academics rarely remember to call on staff for their help in lecturing on certain topics. No listing exists to help academics know about the specialties of the student affairs professionals, and this topic is not a discussable issue in main faculty meetings. For obvious job security issues, staff and faculty still seem to keep unspoken boundaries around their specific qualifications. The exception to this remains the learning community, where the focus is on student learning, and both student affairs and academic affairs share the teaching responsibility for incoming freshman students.

The organizational structure of a small campus may be the biggest barrier to total integrative collaboration. Student affairs professionals are rarely appointed to the same committees or task forces as faculty. Meetings for daily business still take place exclusively: there is an all-faculty meeting monthly and an all-staff meeting monthly, each to the exclusion of the other. It is an observable fact that many discussions in faculty meetings revolve around student issues pertinent to student affairs, yet the discussions often proceed without input or invitation to student affairs professionals to participate, and vice versa.

NEW DIRECTIONS FOR STUDENT SERVICES • DOI: 10.1002/ss

Moving Beyond Boundaries Toward Student Success. As access to higher education increases, so too does the diversity in learners' backgrounds, interests, strengths, preparation, and goals. As a religiously affiliated urban institution, Grand View College draws diverse learners, particularly from the Des Moines metro area and suburbs. In one year alone, Grand View's admission of provisional freshmen has substantially increased while admission to the first-year honors program, Logos, has remained constant. According to Grand View's Fall 2005 New Class Profile, 30.9 percent of the entering freshman class was provisionally admitted to the college. Provisionally admitted students generally come to college with a stigma; at Grand View, they have a high school GPA below a 2.0 or a composite ACT score below 18. This increase in learner diversity is decidedly positive for the educational experience of GVC students. In reality, an increase in the number of provisionally admitted students creates fertile ground for partnerships throughout campus. Faculty members and student development personnel partner to support provisionally admitted students, as well as all Grand View students, through orientation activities, advising and mentoring, and academic support.

All tenure-track faculty members have advising responsibilities. In addition to assisting students with course selection and degree planning, several faculty members and student affairs professionals serve as freshman advisors, providing some of the earliest contacts with first-year students and their families. During summer orientation small-group sessions, first-year advisors discuss topics such as the differences in expectations between high school and college, involvement in organizations and activities, study strategies, and campus resources before beginning conversations on class schedules and degree requirements. These early meetings with students and their families reinforce the notion that academic and student affairs professionals are not limited to stringent job responsibilities. Rather, a general sense of a whole-campus commitment to student needs sets the tone for the academic year.

Academic support during the school year is available for all students inside and beyond the classroom. Tutoring and study tables are coordinated by the campus learning coach, a student development professional. In this structure, course-specific study tables and individual and small-group tutoring are provided as a free resource. Some faculty members also host review sessions. For example, in the fall 2005 semester, a math professor met with students before each test to answer questions and review concepts. The Supplemental Instruction (SI) program, a collaborative effort between academic and student affairs, provides additional support for students enrolled in historically difficult classes.

During the 2006–2007 academic year, living-learning communities further enable academic affairs and student affairs to partner in the education of Grand View students. Called Places of Discovery, these residential communities benefit from faculty and student development mentors who provide educational programming and support. In addition to living on the same floor, students in the learning community take a one-credit leadership development course each semester; a faculty member and a student affairs professional collaborate to coteach the course. The living-learning communities model clearly links academic and student development functions and provides many opportunities for student development staff to further assert themselves as educators while sharing their skills and knowledge with students.

With the support of the Title III grant, Grand View's focus on retention and student success has led to several additional collaborative initiatives currently in place throughout campus. Paramount among these is Grand View's learning communities model, intentionally linking the required new student seminar, taught by academic affairs and student affairs educators, with one or more liberal arts core or major requirement classes. Developmental courses in English and reading strategies are also linked with new student seminar sections for students in need of basic skills review while transitioning to the college environment. The individual teaching a section of the new student seminar also serves as the academic advisor to the same core group of students. This structure allows all seminar instructors to take on multiple roles for student support. During the course of the semester, students view their new student seminar instructors, whether faculty member or student development practitioner, as a teacher, advisor, counselor, advocate, mentor, and campus resource.

A large part of student development's work in any institution occurs behind the scenes, outside the classroom. This is sometimes a preference of the student development professional and sometimes an effect of the campus structure. Astin and Astin (2000) discussed this phenomenon: "Many current structures and policies within our institutions relegate student affairs professionals to the margins in discussions about learning, in part because there is a shared belief that teaching is the sole province of faculty and that learning occurs only within the classroom" (p. 56). Most student development educators concur that learning occurs in all aspects of the student experience. Grand View offers further examples of student affairs professionals taking on formal and informal roles as educators.

In addition to the new student seminar, some student development professionals have experience teaching other formal, credited courses as adjunct instructors in departments such as math and English. Two key administrators, the director of academic advising/Title III retention specialist and the registrar/Title III grant coordinator, maintain faculty status while working in administrative positions. As evidenced by their titles, these individuals have dual roles on campus because of their additional responsibilities in the Title III grant structure. It is obviously helpful for both individuals to have previous academic affairs experience in their current positions; essentially, they link academic affairs to student affairs in campuswide efforts to increase student learning, engagement, and retention. Although a small number of student development professionals teach and a few former faculty members now focus on student affairs and administra-

NEW DIRECTIONS FOR STUDENT SERVICES • DOI: 10.1002/ss

tion, several opportunities exist to further expand student affairs' role as educators and academic affairs' role outside the classroom.

In addition to accepting official teaching roles on campus, GVC student development professionals also collaborate across departments to enhance student success and retention. The Council of Concern, comprising representatives from residence life, athletics, academic success, advising, campus ministry, multicultural programs, and new student programs, meets weekly to discuss student academic and behavioral concerns. The council is frequently called on by faculty with student concerns. The focus of the group is primarily academic success, and because academic success is linked to myriad parts of an individual's life (emotional and physical well-being, outside obligations, financial concerns), collaboration among student development specialties is frequent. Although the Council of Concern is largely successful in its interventions with and academic support of many students, an area of opportunity for partnership exists in its inclusion of representatives from academic affairs. Currently, no professors serve on the committee. Although some in academic affairs have shown interest in assisting the council, the unofficial committee is not considered a faculty committee appointment. Thus, it is difficult for most tenure-track professors to justify their involvement with the council in addition to their official teaching, service, and scholarship obligations.

The Council of Concern was a catalyst for the Academic Success Team (AST). Each spring, four student affairs professionals (the director and assistant director of advising, the learning coach, and the director of academic enrichment) take responsibility for mentoring and tracking second-semester students who were either placed on academic probation or who retained their provisional acceptance to Grand View College after the fall semester. Using a strengths-based approach to intervention, each AST member helps students explore their individual strengths and engages students in discussions and activities that focus on goal setting and behaviors that contribute to academic success. AST members are educators, helping students gain self-reflection, goal-setting, and academic-success skills.

The Student Success Committee is an additional collaborative venture among various facets of student and academic life. Students are also among the committee members. In addition to meeting as a large group, its subcommittees specialize in support for first-year, transfer, and nontraditional learners. As evidenced by the committee's title, the Student Success Committee strives to identify resources for academic success, examine current student support strategies on campus, and develop specific steps to better serve and retain Grand View students.

Whether in student affairs or academic affairs, most educators on campus acknowledge that skills such as critical thinking, questioning, and development of an appreciation for the liberal arts and lifelong learning are not solely nurtured in the GVC classroom. These skills are components of student development's mission in higher education and fundamental to the mission of Grand View College. The transferability of

NEW DIRECTIONS FOR STUDENT SERVICES • DOI: 10.1002/ss

student affairs' expertise to the classroom is becoming increasingly evident on Grand View's campus. Recently, a faculty member teaching human resource management asked the campus's director of internships and new student programs to teach a class session on interviewing techniques. It was important, the professor reasoned, that students learn and practice skills essential for their success as interviewers and interviewees. Another example of this collaboration also comes from the Business Department. To serve the large number of students declaring the business administration major, the Business Department is offering an optional one-credit orientation to the business major and its associated careers. A student development professional from the Career Center facilitates the course, providing another link between academic and student affairs. These are simple and logical uses of a student development professional's time and talents in the classroom setting. It makes seamless the link between student and academic affairs. More curricular partnerships such as this continue to manifest at Grand View College.

Some student affairs professionals also take an active role as resources and educators for those in academic and student affairs positions. The director and assistant director of academic advising educate faculty members and student development staff in monthly advisor in-service training sessions. Topics for training come from a needs assessment as well as anecdotal comments from advisors and quantitative data from advisor assessments completed annually by students. Fifty-minute training sessions with titles such as "Using Student Development Theory in Advising," "Advising Transfer Students," "Intrusive/Developmental Advising," "Advising Students on Academic Probation," and "Legal and Ethical Concerns in Advising" combine information for all faculty advisors and interested professionals with the opportunity for experienced faculty advisors and student affairs practitioners to share strategies and expertise with newer professionals. The Advising Department also provides all campus employees with monthly e-mail tips called "Advice on Advising," which provide concise information on a specific advising issue in addition to an Internet link or reference with additional information. The director and assistant director of advising serve as resources and facilitators for advisor development. They ground their presentations in professional literature on advising and student development theory, finding even greater legitimacy with their audience as they draw on research.

The Center for Excellence in Teaching and Learning (CETL) provides resources and support to develop teaching and advising skills for all professionals on campus. Texts, emerging technological equipment, observation and consultation regarding teaching strategies, and workshops are some of the supplements and services available to student affairs and academic affairs professionals. In addition, the Title III activity director and learning specialist sends out a weekly "Teaching Tips," focusing on topics such as assessment of learning, student engagement, technology in teaching, and student motivation. Although these topics are often presented in relation to teaching, it is notable that each is integral to the work of a student development professional as well. It is important for student development professionals to assert their roles as educators. It is equally vital for these professionals to use educational resources such as "Teaching Tips" and the offerings of the CETL to strengthen their effectiveness in multiple roles.

As a church-affiliated institution, Grand View College continues to reinforce the Lutheran practice of service throughout the student body. A director of multicultural and community outreach position exists in the Student Life Office. This vital link connects students to service opportunities in the surrounding community. Learning through service, whether through a volunteer experience or as a class requirement, is a powerful opportunity for partnerships among all campus employees, students, and the greater community. Academic and student affairs professionals can partner with community agencies and organizations in their specialty areas to provide a connection to different academic disciplines in the service setting. Connections to service opportunities in career interest areas can aid in vocational exploration. Students are asked to reflect on their service activities, resulting in skill development in writing, critical thinking, and discussion. This reflection also provides the opportunity to experience interconnectedness with peers as well as local and campus communities. Service learning opportunities present the foundation for the very essence of the college mission (Grand View College, 2004). The first sentence of the mission summarizes the importance of the theme of service: "Grand View College engages, equips, and empowers students to fulfill their ambitions and to serve society" (p. 5).

Conclusion

Like many small colleges, Grand View continues to experience successes and face challenges in campus collaborations. Student affairs educators, by their very titles, are teachers; the challenge of presenting themselves in that light to students and faculty members continues. Faculty often remain unchallenged to open the boundaries of their job descriptions to include partnerships with student affairs professionals. Student affairs professionals sometimes are all too willing to engage in "unequal" partnerships. Yet strides are clearly being made on this small campus, and support from administration is high for these collaborative efforts to continue. Instead of smaller campuses vying to model themselves after larger universities, perhaps larger campuses need to look for inspiration and innovative ideas about collaborative efforts from smaller campuses like Grand View College.

References

Astin, A., and Astin, H. *Leadership Reconsidered: Engaging Higher Education in Social Change.* Battle Creek, Mich.: Kellogg Foundation, 2000.

Grand View College. *Grand View College 2004–2006 Catalog.* 2004. http://mycampus.gvc. edu/catalog0406/html/catalog0406.html. Accessed Oct. 23, 2005.

NEW DIRECTIONS FOR STUDENT SERVICES • DOI: 10.1002/ss

Grand View College. *Fall 2005 New Class Profile.* 2005. http://mycampus.gvc.edu/
fsresource/enrollmentmgmt/data/fall05profile.pdf. Accessed Dec. 2, 2005.

Jacoby, B. "Partnerships for Service Learning." In J. H. Schuh and E. J. Whitt (eds.), *Creating Successful Partnerships Between Academic and Student Affairs.* New Directions for
Student Services, no. 87. San Francisco: Jossey-Bass, 1999.

Kantor, D., and Lehr, W. *Inside the Family.* San Francisco: Jossey-Bass, 1975.

Kinzie, J., and Kuh, G. "Going Deep: Learning from Campuses That Share Responsibility for Student Success." *About Campus,* 2004, 9(5).

Kuh, G., and Banta, T. "Faculty-Student Affairs Collaboration on Assessment." *About
Campus,* 2000, 4(6).

Magolda, P. M. "Proceed with Caution: Uncommon Wisdom About Academic and Student Affairs Partnerships." *About Campus,* 2005, 9(6).

Schroeder, C., Minor, F., and Tarkow, T. "Freshman Interest Groups: Partnerships for
Promoting Student Success." In J. H. Schuh and E. J. Whitt (eds.), *Creating Successful Partnerships Between Academic and Student Affairs.* New Directions for Student Services, no. 87. San Francisco: Jossey-Bass, 1999.

Schuh, J. "Guiding Principles for Evaluating Student and Academic Affairs Partnerships."
In J. H. Schuh and E. J. Whitt (eds.), *Creating Successful Partnerships Between Aca-
demic and Student Affairs.* New Directions for Student Services, no. 87. San Francisco:
Jossey-Bass, 1999.

Senge, P. *The Fifth Discipline Fieldbook.* New York: Bantam Doubleday Dell, 1994.

Westfall, S. "Partnerships to Connect In- and Out-of-Class Experiences." In J. H. Schuh
and E. J. Whitt (eds.), *Creating Successful Partnerships Between Academic and Student
Affairs.* New Directions for Student Services, no. 87. San Francisco: Jossey-Bass, 1999.

GRETA DEGEN *is assistant professor in nursing at Grand View College in Des
Moines, Iowa.*

ERIN SHELDAHL *is the former assistant director of academic advising at Grand
View College in Des Moines, Iowa. Currently she is a seventh-grade writing
instructor for Hoffman Academy in Houston, Texas.*

6

Student affairs professionals are part of a great transformation in higher education—dynamic programs that promote student learning in classroom and cocurricular settings. They can share their experiences with others, but as they become "scholarly practitioners" they can also create valuable knowledge and understanding for colleges and universities.

Articulation, Communication, Dissemination: Sharing Your Experiences with Others

Emily L. Moore, J. Herman Blake

Colleges and universities are some of the most important cultural institutions in American society. Their long existence is one testimony to their fundamental importance. Many of them have celebrated their bicentennials and sesquicentennials, while many others are well past their centennials. They are firmly rooted in cultural traditions and practices that are recognized as important parts of America. The research they conduct, the education they offer, and the social services they perform are economic and social foundations of America. Inside very stable academic structures, dynamic and rapid changes are under way. Their research and scholarly missions ensure that change is a constant in the framework of stable cultural patterns. Social and demographic changes at both national and international levels require additional changes in our institutions.

The combination of cultural stability and dynamic change presents unique challenges for student affairs. As institutions respond to the challenges of the new millennium, student affairs leaders will be expected to exhibit greater and greater professionalism. This expectation is seen in the transformation of student affairs, as professionals become active and often central participants in student learning. This participation will become more intentional and cover the entire range of student experiences from the initial contact upon arrival on campus through learning communities, first-year programs, and classroom activities.

New Directions for Student Services, no. 117, Spring 2007   © Wiley Periodicals, Inc.
Published online in Wiley InterScience (www.interscience.wiley.com) • DOI: 10.1002/ss.233

The new professionalism in student affairs will also create expectations that participants will share their developing insights and understandings beyond their particular campus. The professional exchange of the new knowledge will be an important part of the practice of institutional change in the cultural framework of institutional stability. We believe student affairs professionals can offer insights of great importance to higher education as a result of their unique work.

We can approach the process of educating other academic divisions by considering the stages that result in the dissemination of new knowledge. In this chapter we discuss strategies for articulating, analyzing, communicating, and ultimately, disseminating new insights and understandings.

Articulation

The articulation phase involves capturing new experiences as soon as possible after they occur. It is important to make a record of the activities and programs while the memory is fresh. It is even more important to record the thoughts, ideas, and reflections of the participants shortly after events occur. This permits one to record particular thoughts before they fade with the passage of time. We always keep a small notebook in a pocket or purse to make cryptic notes that can be expanded later in a journal or diary. We have found the journaling process of great value in recording new experiences.

Classroom reflections are valuable approaches for assessing as well as recording new experiences. In our undergraduate classes we often reserve the last ten minutes of each class for free writing. While students reflect on the particular class or their learning experience and its meaning, we write our personal assessment of the class and our reflections about what worked and why. We reflect on our own performance as well as student participation. There is no effort to structure these writing experiences; we allow the mind to range free over the past session. Students may submit their thoughts without identification if they wish. Submission is not required. These personal reflections are retained in our records for future review. Sometimes they are repeated and expanded in our journals.

We also recommend that professionals set aside several periods each week to record their experiences and reflections in a diary. It is very important that these articulations occur regularly and frequently. Key events or ideas can be lost quickly as new experiences displace memories. We cannot stress too greatly the long-term value of writing, reflection, and journaling to capture impressions and reflections as they take place. Over a period of several months a substantial amount of valuable information can be amassed. The aggregation of recorded activities and reflections will eventually become a strong foundation for the analytical process that will move the professional experience to a much higher level.

New Directions for Student Services • DOI: 10.1002/ss

of the two, an intimate and intuitive knowledge of the mater-
it maximum flexibility in pedagogy. Ultimately a successful pre-
ill involve the "scholarly practitioner" effectively connecting
ience through the complex prisms of personality, situation, and
-material. When one has maximum knowledge of all three, one
the pedagogical strategy that is most comfortable, and then
ebb and flow of time and events in the workshop. The material
rable; with a good understanding of oneself as presenter and the
recipient the possibility of maximum learning is enhanced.
ways valuable to include assessment strategies to determine if the
ion goals have been achieved. This assessment can range from a
ire to written reflections and essays or verbal feedback. We pre-
reflections and essays that are unsigned because they give us
ered feedback. The circle is completed when the assessment and
ecome a new step in the articulation process. Regardless of what
employed, effective pedagogy always includes assessment and
mechanisms.

dy from a Career

r is a case study in the integration of academic and student affairs
lue of scholarly approaches to our work. In spite of years of success
rams that fostered student learning, retention, and graduation, it was
we analyzed our most recent success that we came to appreciate the
ur understanding. An intentional program of articulation, analysis,
munication led us to develop concepts and theories that were read-
ent but unrecognized.
en we joined a Midwestern land-grant university in 1998 we became
used on articulation of our experiences. In our classes we engaged in
able reflection through writing and assessments. We also wrote inde-
ly about our experiences. When we conducted workshops we would
ly conclude with written reflections by the participants as well as our-
ver time we accumulated a considerable number of descriptions, dis-
, and assessments of our work from a wide variety of individuals.
ddition to our course work we were deeply involved with under-
e cocurricular programs that promoted active student involvement
learning. Student staff in these programs wrote extensive reflections
meetings—describing the events as well as their interpretations and
l sentiments. We also wrote about our experience of the meetings
udents—describing at length our impressions and personal reflec-
n this manner we amassed a considerable amount of information
pinions and ideas as well as events.
multaneously we conducted a regular review of the research and
rly literature on student learning. Although many of these reviews
ded with preparation for teaching, many of them were for personal

Analysis

The analytical phase involves two separate but overlapping activities. The descriptions of reflections and programs should be carefully reviewed, expanded, and corrected. This should occur repeatedly, for each reading will inspire new thoughts about past and future programs. In this review process one is searching for recurring themes and patterns in the material. These patterns can then be organized into summaries based initially on either chronological trends or logical patterns. The goal is to move beyond a mere "show-and-tell" description of events toward generalized summaries that transform the descriptive reflections into analytical and even predictive conceptual frameworks. The review of the journals and classroom assessments is a search for general patterns and themes.

Simultaneously, student affairs professionals actively engaged in the teaching-learning process must conduct regular reviews and analyses of the growing research literature on student learning. Although a large number of publications analyze student learning, over time some will be recognized as summative and particularly valuable. In reviewing this literature the quest is to identify substantive concepts, hypotheses, and theories that give depth and meaning to the review of one's own journals and classroom assessments. The application of the more abstract formulations from the literature to the more personalized formulations of the student affairs professional will result in a productive set of ideas that are informed by experience and confirmed by the research of others.

The ultimate goal in the analytical process is to do more than describe the outcomes of activities and programs. The goal is to develop analytical concepts and theories that will explain *why* a particular outcome resulted from the activity, and *why* other outcomes did not occur. The analytical process will also permit predictive statements about outcomes that can occur in other venues or under different conditions. Such explanations will lead others to seek to replicate desirable outcomes in teaching and learning.

Communication: New Ideas and Insights

Over time the articulation and analysis processes will lead to insights and understandings worthy of wider consideration. This is the point when professionals should begin to specify their new knowledge in essays and papers that can ultimately be shared with others. The most valuable essays will go beyond descriptions of events. Thoughtful and insightful analysis will lead to deeper understanding and expansion of widely shared concepts. As these essays are revised and improved they will lead to new concepts and theoretical formulations. This is the point at which the essays are ready to be shared with wider audiences, initially on campus or in regional conferences, but ultimately nationally.

Like the reviews of the journals and assessments, the resultant essays must be given time to develop in one's mind. It is very important to give new essays repeated revisions and improvements over a period of several months. Ultimately, lasting contributions to student affairs as an academic and intellectual process will come from seasoned and mature contributions from professionals who are able to combine their intense involvement with students with an equally intense pattern of reflection and analysis.

Even though we describe the processes of articulation, analysis, and communication in discrete segments, they are in fact enmeshed with each other. In reality the professional will be constantly moving between the three phases because the different parts will inform and improve one another. It is a very dynamic process.

This is all part of student affairs professionals becoming more intentional in their focus on student learning and the new knowledge that develops as a result. In the process the professional moves beyond the practice of student affairs into the realm of scholarly practitioner—that is, a professional who does critical study of his or her work toward the goal of discovering and disseminating new insights about students and the structure of higher education. These insights are ultimately summarized as new concepts and theories about research, teaching, and learning.

Dissemination

The process of sharing new concepts and theories permits critical feedback about developing knowledge. Such critical feedback will allow further refinement of the developing concepts and theories. In their most embryonic form the ideas can be shared in staff meetings and campus seminars. Eventually, however, it will be appropriate to seek larger audiences.

Initially we recommend professionals begin to share their scholarly productivity beyond the campus with peers in statewide and regional programs sponsored by professional associations. As the ideas are refined they can be submitted for consideration at national and international conferences.

Verbal and poster presentations at such conferences will challenge professionals to craft their scholarship into precise and well-defined formulations. Once again we are focusing on presentations that go far beyond the descriptive level. Although interesting, descriptive accounts do not advance learning or deepen understanding. To achieve these goals in verbal and poster presentations, professionals must have a strong sense of the vision and mission underlying the scholarly products. From this base they can go into a brief description of events, but place their major focus on outcomes and an explanation of why these particular outcomes occurred. It will be much easier to present the material verbally or in a poster if there is clarity about vision and mission.

As the number of professionals wit learning as well as intuitive knowledge a ination can take place in larger venues. able insights worthy of consideration in e national presentations as well as general v

Workshops—sessions that run for fo be most productive if professionals give a cal strategies they will use in the sessions submitting proposals for conference pres strategies are salient.

Principles for Preparation

Three basic principles should govern how pr ference presentations are prepared: (1) knov ence, and (3) know your material. These thr pedagogical approach in any circumstance.

In assessing one's presentation skills it i nesses as well as strengths. Although the pri strengths, a thoughtful pedagogy will minimiz very good at the lecture approach, whereas oth sational or discussion approach. Neither is prefe if the planned session calls for the one at which deficit can be overcome through reliance on copr sion to minimize the weak points and maximize t presentations in different settings and receives fee standing of one's strong points. Regardless of circ should be based on the solid foundation of the vi the work. For many years we have sought to copr mize the weaknesses of the other. We have found

A second key to successful workshops and to know the audience. Although this information every effort should be made to gain advance unde Some—but not all—of the questions for conside their motivation for participation? Are they reall of the workshop? Do they really seek to know an tation? Are they present because they have altern prevail? Are they coming because of some requir to gain continuing education credits rather than their presence totally unrelated to the workshop? tation and subsequent discussion these and other reactions and interactions.

The third principle is to know one's material. results of one's own research and studies, the res

combinatio
ial will perm
sentation w
with the au
information
can develo
manage the
is the deliv
audience a

It is al
disseminat
questionna
fer writter
unencumb
feedback
strategy is
feedback

Case Stu

Our caree
and the v
with prog
not until
depth of
and com
ily appar

Wh
more foo
consider
pendent
frequent
selves.
cussion

In
graduat
in thei
on the
person
with s
tions.
about

Si
schola
coinci

and professional growth. In the cocurricular support groups we had student staff review other literature as a part of their leadership development. The literature reviews and our own reflections were combined into a series of papers we delivered at professional meetings—regionally, nationally, and internationally. We also conducted workshops on our findings with faculty and student affairs groups in different venues, seeking their feedback and critical reactions.

As we continued to share our ideas with others—reflecting the literature as well as our own experiences—we came to the realization that ideas and concepts we thought were well understood and predictive were also limited. This was surprising to us because we thought we had good knowledge of what worked and an understanding of why it worked.

In our most recent experience we saw a substantial increase in black student six-year graduation rates (48 percent between 1998 and 2005). Although gratified by this outcome, it was beyond our expectations. We are now in the process of reconsidering all our material and previous writings. As we compare the most recent outcomes with our reflections, student writings, and the literature we find ourselves developing new concepts and theoretical formulations that we believe will better explain such dynamic improvement. What is more, these new concepts will be more precise, predictive, and replicable. We expect to make substantial contributions to student affairs and academic programs in higher education. Our future work will focus on the integration of student and academic affairs, the promotion of student learning in holistic environments, and strategies for success in retention and graduation.

Conclusion

Student affairs professionals are in the early phase of an exciting and dynamic process of change. They are positioned to accumulate substantial information about the experiences of undergraduates involved in comprehensive approaches to student learning. Through a process of sharing their experiences with others as discussed in this chapter, professionals can become scholarly practitioners with profound insights into how they can teach more effectively in the academy and promote higher levels of student learning.

EMILY L. MOORE is professor emerita of educational leadership and policy studies at Iowa State University. In January 2007 she was appointed provost and vice president for academic affairs at Dillard University in New Orleans, Louisiana.

J. HERMAN BLAKE is professor emeritus of sociology and educational leadership and policy studies at Iowa State University, and scholar-in-residence and director of the Sea Islands Institute at the University of South Carolina, Beaufort.

NEW DIRECTIONS FOR STUDENT SERVICES • DOI: 10.1002/ss

7

Professionals with responsibilities for student affairs can play a major role in the increasing emphasis on academic achievement, student learning, and retention. The outlines of future perspectives on professionalism and personal development can be found in examples from the recent past. The new developments will combine historical perspectives with insights from ongoing changes.

The Crucial Role of Student Affairs Professionals in the Learning Process

J. Herman Blake

In the first decade of a new millennium three propositions are basic to any consideration of the future role of student affairs professionals in higher education:

1. Demographic changes in the larger society and on college campuses mandate a much more comprehensive and creative approach to serving students.
2. Colleges and universities must place even greater emphasis on retention and graduation of students than they place on recruiting new matriculates.
3. Developing research shows that the primary key to retention through graduation is a strong emphasis on student learning; this emphasis is rapidly becoming a sine qua non.

Although many colleges place considerable emphasis on attractive residences, technology, athletic facilities, and cocurricular programs in recruiting new students, the evidence is clear that ultimate success in retention to graduation requires increased emphasis on academic achievement through active student involvement in the learning process.

Given these propositions, student affairs professionals would do well to look to strategies for increasing academic achievement and student learning as keys to a creative and efficacious future for the profession. Beyond strategies for students per se, a new approach also implies new perspectives

NEW DIRECTIONS FOR STUDENT SERVICES, no. 117, Spring 2007 © Wiley Periodicals, Inc.
Published online in Wiley InterScience (www.interscience.wiley.com) • DOI: 10.1002/ss.234

on professionalism and paradigm shifts in the conceptualization of professionals with student affairs responsibilities.

An Emphasis on Student Learning

In four decades of administration, teaching, research, and leadership, I have served in a wide range of academic institutions, always placing a strong emphasis on increasing the retention and graduation of underrepresented minority students through academic achievement. The creative participation of student affairs professionals in all of these programs has been an important part of increasing levels of success.

Initial Efforts in the Teaching-Learning Process. During the 1970s as a professor as well as principal academic-administrative officer in an undergraduate residential college in a Research I university, I began to explore initial efforts in directly involving student affairs professionals in the teaching-learning process. About one-third of our students were African American, American Indian, and Latino. Although the regular tenure-track faculty were responsible for class offerings, the entire student affairs staff played major supplementary roles.

The goal was to create a social and intellectual environment of high academic expectations of students through carefully crafted programs in which student affairs and academic affairs were thoroughly interwoven.

The director of student activities was a full member of the college curriculum committee and developed an out-of-class program that complemented and promoted the classroom learning. This was an early articulation of the "cocurricular" concept. A psychological counselor enrolled in mathematics and science classes with the students to create a symbiotic relation between counseling sessions with students on test anxiety and their classroom experiences. In addition, the director of housing, the bursar, and clerical staff joined faculty as coleaders of discussion sections of core courses. As a result students found that those with whom they dealt on administrative and personal matters were also those they saw in the classrooms working with them on academic issues. In their professional interaction with students, academic issues would often be discussed. Student affairs professionals became teachers by design rather than default. The academic emphasis that permeated every aspect of the college led to higher levels of student academic achievement and retention to graduation. We created a college culture centered around student learning.

Creating an Environment of High Expectation. During the 1980s, as president of a small African-American liberal arts college in the Deep South, the process of intentionally creating a total environment of high academic expectations continued. Working together, faculty and enrollment management staff created a reading list of books required of all entering students the summer before they enrolled. Shortly after new students moved into the residence halls we opened the year with a general convocation in which a panel of faculty and administrators (including student affairs staff) discussed the key books. New students got their first academic experience before they got their first campus meal. The next day, as a part of orientation, students were required to write a general essay on one of the books—and student affairs staff wrote a narrative evaluation of the essay. New students who had taken the time to read the books during the summer found themselves at an academic advantage over those who had ignored the assignment. The message we conveyed stressed learning as the primary activity and goal of the college environment, and learning would also take place outside of the classroom and traditional course requirements. In the required freshman core course the infusion process continued with movies and other cocurricular activities that emerged from classroom requirements but were available to the entire student body. The idea was to create campus discussions of issues and ideas the students were considering in the classrooms. In some cases professional staff also joined faculty as coinstructors in the core course.

Addressing the Challenge of Nontraditional Students. In a large urban public university (Research I) in the 1990s, I was responsible for leading the effort to address the academic needs of eight thousand "nontraditional" commuting students. The challenge was to integrate an incredible range of diverse interests and social conditions into an effective program that would promote academic achievement, retention, and ultimately, graduation. Over a period of years we transformed an advising and counseling unit known as University Division into a lower-division academic program. This required vision and leadership from the faculty as well as student affairs. With their cooperation we formed learning teams in which faculty joined with academic advisors, peer counselors, and librarians to create a supportive unit for every class in the new academic program. The goal was to develop a safety net for students that promoted their academic goals through high expectations and their active involvement in the learning process. The creation of learning teams of faculty and student affairs professionals as partners promoted an academic culture in an environment where the social conditions were unique and unlike any of our previous experiences. The faculty-student affairs partnership was crucial to this successful program.

Integrating Academic Programs and Cocurricular Activities. As the new century opened I continued my work in a large (twenty-five thousand students), rural, land-grant Research I university. With the experience and knowledge of three decades in diverse academic settings I integrated academic programs and cocurricular activities that resulted in our highest rates of success in retention to graduation of diverse students.

Comprehensive programs of academic courses and faculty-student research coordinated with the cocurriculum extended far beyond the classrooms—integrating administrators and student affairs professionals in creative ways. In one program, student support groups focused on improving learning and study skills were linked to specific courses. Faculty, staff, and administrators found that attendance at the meetings of the support groups permitted more effective interaction with students than would take place in their offices or laboratories. Indeed, members of the counseling staff found that participation in the meetings of the student support groups led to discussions—and often private meetings—with students who would not come to their offices.

In another instance I taught a special section of the class Introduction to Sociology. The course was limited to thirty to forty students—recruited to ensure a diverse class. Besides including a good mix of racial and ethnic groups, the class had one student who had just returned from active duty in Iraq, another scheduled for deployment at the end of the semester, and a third who was engaged to a soldier in combat in Iraq. It was a very eclectic group. The meetings were held in the residence hall where most of them lived, and the hall director as well as a senior-level housing staff member were active participants in the course. Once each week I met with these two student affairs professionals for about an hour before class to discuss the assignments, the students, their academic performance, and how we might improve their time on task as well as their learning. What is more, the course met in the late afternoon as a way of encouraging students to go to dinner in small groups and continue the discussions in the cafeteria. We also used other strategies to actively engage students in their learning experience. Student evaluations of the course and their learning revealed that we not only accomplished our goals but the positive impact was far greater than we expected. Students learned sociology—the course goal—but they also learned a great deal about cultural and social differences, as well as respect for individuals regardless of social characteristics.

As a consequence of these and other programs from 1998 to 2005, the six-year graduation rate of African-American students increased by 48 percent to the highest level in the institution's history.

In every venue success was not individual, it was not strictly a result of faculty status of distinguished colleagues or administrative position, nor was it solely a consequence of the actions of student affairs professionals. The opportunity to build meaningful programs of mutual support and cooperation between academic affairs, faculty involved in research as well as teaching, and student affairs professionals in a context of high expectations for academic achievement resulted in higher and higher levels of student success. As I continue to analyze these experiences and their outcomes— particularly for underrepresented minority students—I realize there were two key features in every situation: (1) a campus culture or subculture of high expectations for students emerged from the collaboration and intentional efforts of different campus constituencies that usually operated separately from each other; and (2) ultimately students expanded their sense of self beyond the identities they brought into the academy, shaping their views of academic life and of others as well as of themselves. These expanded identities were even more complex and combined previous modes with strong identification with academic domains. What was often a conflict-oriented or adversarial process between students and the academic environment became more a culture of cooperation, growth, and learning. The active participation of student affairs professionals was crucial to these extraordinary changes.

The Changing and Dynamic Role of Student Affairs Professionals in the Teaching-Learning Process

Presidents of colleges and universities face daunting challenges in meeting the needs of an increasingly diverse student body and fulfilling an expansive institutional mission. As they recognize the significance of academic achievement for student retention and graduation they will seek to create social environments that expand the traditional emphasis on extracurricular activities to incorporate a greater focus on student learning. Student affairs professionals will be expected to play key roles in the transformation of the campus environment. Although the traditional focus on activities and programs will continue, the traditional roles of student affairs personnel will face significant changes.

Initially, these new expectations will not fit easily into a job description, other than a call for professional growth and development as a result of new knowledge and understanding and the articulation of new issues in institutional mission. These expectations will require a new conceptualization by student affairs professionals—indeed, a new sense of self-identity as well as an intentional recalibration of their efforts with changes in campus missions and strategic plans. They must begin to envision themselves as promoters of learning and academic achievement in virtually everything they do with students.

Increasingly, administrators will assess student activities and the interaction of student affairs professionals for their learning potential—whether they are formal or informal outcomes. Responsive staff will recognize they do more teaching in their offices, in the residence halls, and in student unions than they ever realized. Even a discussion with a student about a professor or a course can be turned into a teaching experience if it is consciously seen as raising the student's academic performance and the amount of time spent on learning. Such an approach will require a paradigm shift for student affairs professionals.

Becoming Professionals. As we look to the future through the past we envision student affairs professionals as individuals who place much more emphasis on their professional status than on student affairs. Thus they will become *professionals who practice student affairs* rather than the reverse. As such incumbents must view themselves in terms of the mission, values, and goals of the institution, and reconsider how they can promote student learning through their own professional growth. This requires individuals to become more confident in their personal ability to learn and grow and promote that process among students. Such professionals have assigned responsibilities that bring them into close and very personal contact with students. As a result of their enhanced professionalism they will come to develop new ways to enhance student learning through student activities.

When I taught the sociology class in a residence hall with the hall director as a full participant in the teaching process, the weekly planning meetings became seminars on how teaching, learning, and student affairs could be integrated into a seamless web of programmed activities. The hall director used knowledge of the students' personal circumstances to individualize the teaching process and create greater student involvement in the class sessions. In addition the hall director worked with me to create assignments that allowed students to infuse their residential life with study and research sessions that extended the classroom throughout the residence hall and affected even students who were not enrolled in the class. There was no preconceived plan about how the class might work. It was a dynamic process of analysis and assessment of the class and ourselves as class leaders, and constantly focused on student learning. The hall director had to be a professional with skills that went far beyond mine as a professor and who could use those skills and insights to increase my understanding, student active involvement in the course, and ultimately, student learning. Students completed course evaluations that showed the class went far beyond their expectations of a traditional introductory course, and they believed their learning had significantly increased as a consequence. There was nothing in the position description or written expectations of a hall director that led to such a positive outcome. It was the consequence of the growth and insights of a professional who was also a hall director. In the future role of student affairs the emphasis on professionalism as well as personal growth of incumbents will become an important part of the new paradigm.

Even on small campuses the range of activities developed and promoted by student affairs is extraordinary. It has been long understood that the groups and activities are an important part of a balanced and productive college environment. Although many activities and programs should rightfully focus on enabling students to enjoy their undergraduate experience apart from academic pressures, professionals with student affairs responsibilities can help their charges connect the student activities to the academic expectations in such a way that learning becomes an intrinsic part of the campus cocurriculum.

In the first example given in this chapter, when the director of student activities in a small college was invited by faculty to join the curriculum committee, the goal was to build a creative bridge between academic and student affairs. The professional seized the opportunity and built a very effective program as the result of an appreciation of how student activities could become more learning-centered. The cocurriculum that resulted made specific links between the two arenas. In a biology course that focused on the study of cancer the professor and the professional worked together to organize a series of student presentations on their research to the entire college community in a special lecture series titled "The Biology of Cancer." The presentations were very popular with students. Student presenters became more known and respected by their peers and the subsequent discussions in the residence halls and cafeteria extended the learning arena far beyond the classroom. The resultant increase in knowledge and confidence of the student presenters as well as the general affirmation of their peers helped create a culture of learning and academic achievement in the college.

The paradigm shift here involved a greater sense of professionalism on the part of the faculty member as well as the staff member. However, it took a creative approach from the student affairs professional to show the professor how the two cultures could be integrated into an expanded learning environment. When both individuals saw that cooperation would lead to enhanced student learning they were able to create an academic environment that extended beyond the classroom. The capacity to transcend the student affairs limits was the mark of a gifted professional with responsibility for student activities.

Thinking Creatively. Given the unique mission of different institutions it is inappropriate to specify how student programs can become more learning-centered. What is appropriate is to recognize that student affairs staff who grow into a new identity—as professionals who have student affairs responsibilities—will begin to recognize the learning potential in many of their traditional programs. Through creative thinking resulting from enhanced emphasis on their professional growth and development they will see how to meet their traditional responsibilities in much more effective, learning-centered ways. The same example presented earlier in the chapter will illustrate this point. In two different institutions we found psychological counselors challenged by the reluctance of minority students to visit them in their offices. However, when one counselor enrolled in a mathematics class, and another regularly attended luncheon meetings of student support groups, they found students more willing to approach them in these more neutral settings. In both cases the psychological counselors participated in academically oriented programs and found they were able to establish connections that eventually resulted in private sessions with students in their offices. The professionals had to change their way of thinking about their responsibilities. When they became more directly involved in student learning programs they reached more students. They claimed this was an effective way to extend the reach of their offices.

Recent developments in the organization of academic programs that are more inclusive also require an expanded emphasis on professionalism in the practice of student affairs. In these developing programs student affairs can be pivotal if incumbents are willing to meet the challenge of professional change and growth. The development of learning communities, programs for "students in transition," service learning, and other efforts will present challenging opportunities for professional growth by student affairs personnel. In most if not all of these developments the emphasis on teamwork, cooperation, and integrated programs open new and creative opportunities for professionals with expertise in student affairs to make extraordinary contributions. Student affairs strategies that are often second nature can be expanded to produce learning outcomes if incumbents are willing to expand their thinking through growing professionalism. As a result they can enhance and often transform traditional thinking by faculty about how student learning can be enhanced. Although it is often difficult for faculty members focused on teaching their disciplines to listen to others, effective and creative professionals in student affairs can help these faculty make a greater impact in their teaching with the insights that come from their heightened professionalism.

Conclusion

As we consider the future role of professionals with responsibilities for student affairs in the teaching and learning process, two salient but contradictory proverbs can give us predictive insights.

The philosopher and poet Algernon Swinburne once stated, "All our past proclaims our future." As we look to the recent past to see outlines of the future we are reminded that student affairs emerged out of the reluctance of faculty to become involved in the "hands-on" aspect of college student life. It is clear that the teaching-learning role of professionals in student affairs will involve new and creative combinations of the hands-on/hands-off process. In some respects the "future" role of professionals in student affairs will be something like "back to the future."

The wisdom of an African proverb, offering another perspective, is also salient: "You don't build a house for yesterday's rains." The emphasis on new dimensions of professionalism is crucial because the students of today, and even more, those of tomorrow are very different from those of yesterday. They are much more diverse in race, religion, ethnicity, lifestyle, and many other ways. As we focus on increased student learning as well as a greater sense of "community within diversity," professionals will have to transcend many aspects of the renewed past as they build an unpredictable future for students.

Effective and creative professionals with student affairs responsibilities will embrace the future while remaining deeply rooted in the past. The challenges are exciting and invigorating.

J. HERMAN BLAKE is professor emeritus of sociology and educational leadership and policy studies at Iowa State University, and scholar-in-residence and director of the Sea Islands Institute, University of South Carolina, Beaufort.

NEW DIRECTIONS FOR STUDENT SERVICES • DOI: 10.1002/ss

INDEX

Alschuler, A. S., 13, 15, 16
Approachability, 7
Arthur, G., 1, 13, 24
Assessment and feedback, 8–9
Astin, A. W., 8, 14, 26, 52
Astin, H., 52
Authority, classroom, 7

Ball, D., 13
Barr, R., 27
Baxter Magolda, M. B., 8, 16
Beaumont, E., 9
Benjamin, M, 1, 13, 24, 39
Blake, J. H., 2, 4, 10, 57, 63, 65, 72
Blimling, G. S., 13, 15, 16, 18
Bloland, P. A., 15, 16
Brown, R. D., 4

Chickering, A. W., 5
Chrystal, L. L., 39
Classroom authority, 7
Classroom reflections, 58
Cohen, D. K., 13
Colby, A., 9
Conference presentations, 60–62
Convocation, 18
Creative thinking, 71–72
Curriculum development, 31–32

Degen, G. M., 2, 48, 56
Dewey, J., 36, 37
Dissemination of knowledge: analysis, 59; articulation phase, 58; conclusions on, 63; insights and essays, 59–60; at workshops, 60–62

Earnest, K., 1, 13, 24, 39
Ellertson, S., 1, 35, 46
Elmore, R., 5
Erlich, T., 9
Evans, N. J., 4, 8, 35

Fidler, P. P., 28
First weeks of first year: common activities during, 16–19; conclusions on, 23; importance of, 16; involvement and engagement for, 14–15; location of activities for, 15; sample curriculum

for, 19–23; student affairs educators and, 15–16
First-year experience movement, 28–29
Forney, D. S., 35

Gabelnick, F., 36, 37
Gamson, Z., 5
Gardner, J. N., 28
GI Bill, 26
Gordon, V. N., 28
Grand View College, 50–55
Greater Expectations, 27
Grube, S., 39
Gruenewald, D., 1, 13, 24
Guido-DiBrito, F., 35

Hamrick, F. A., 4, 8
Hunter, M.S., 1, 25, 34

Involvement and engagement, benefits of, 14–15
Iowa State model, 19–23

Jacoby, B., 49
Jones, T., 28
Journaling, 58

Kantor, D., 49
Karnok, K., 10
Keeling, R., 4, 15, 27
King, P. M., 13, 16
King, T., 2
Kinzie, J., 14, 16, 23, 26, 48
Kuh, G. D., 8, 14, 16, 23, 26, 48

Learning communities, 32–33, 35–45
Learning Community National Learning Commons Web site, 44
Lehr, W., 49
Levine Laufgraben, J., 40
Light, R. J., 26

MacGregor, J., 36, 37
Magolda, P. M., 49
Marsh, R., 1, 11
Matthews, R. S., 36, 37
Meiklejohn, A., 36
Minor, F., 49
Moore, E. L., 1, 2, 4, 6, 11, 57, 63

73

SS111   **Gender Identity and Sexual Orientation: Research, Policy, and Personal Perspectives**
Ronni L. Sanlo
Lesbian, gay, bisexual, and transgender people have experienced homophobia, discrimination, exclusion, and marginalization in the academy, from subtle to overt. Yet LGBT people have been a vital part of the history of American higher education. This volume describes current issues, research, and policies, and it offers ways for institutions to support and foster the success of LGBT students, faculty, and staff.
ISBN: 0-7879-8328-4

SS110   **Developing Social Justice Allies**
Robert D. Reason, Ellen M. Broido, Tracy L. Davis, Nancy J. Evans
Social justice allies are individuals from dominant groups (for example, whites, heterosexuals, men) who work to end the oppression of target group members (people of color, homosexuals, women). Student affairs professionals have a history of philosophical commitment to social justice, and this volume strives to provide the theoretical foundation and practical strategies to encourage the development of social justice and civil rights allies among students and colleagues.
ISBN: 0-7879-8077-3

SS109   **Serving Native American Students**
Mary Jo Tippeconnic Fox, Shelly C. Lowe, George S. McClellan
The increasing Native American enrollment on campuses nationwide is something to celebrate; however, the retention rate for Native American students is the lowest in higher education, a point of tremendous concern. This volume's authors—most of them Native American—address topics such as enrollment trends, campus experiences, cultural traditions, student services, ignorance about Indian country issues, expectations of tribal leaders and parents, and other challenges and opportunities encountered by Native students.
ISBN: 0-7879-7971-6

SS108   **Using Entertainment Media in Student Affairs Teaching and Practice**
Deanna S. Forney, Tony W. Cawthon
Reaching all students may require going beyond traditional methods, especially in the out-of-classroom environments typical to student affairs. Using films, music, television shows, and popular books can help students learn. This volume—good for both practitioners and educators—shares effective approaches to using entertainment media to facilitate understanding of general student development, multiculturalism, sexual orientation, gender issues, leadership, counseling, and more.
ISBN: 0-7879-7926-0

SS107   **Developing Effective Programs and Services for College Men**
Gar E. Kellom
This volume's aim is to better understand the challenges facing college men, particularly at-risk men. Topics include enrollment, retention, academic performance, women's college perspectives, men's studies perspectives, men's health issues, emotional development, and spirituality. Delivers recommendations and examples about programs and services that improve college men's learning experiences and race, class, and gender awareness.
ISBN: 0-7879-7772-1

SS106   **Serving the Millennial Generation**
Michael D. Coomes, Robert DeBard
Focuses on the next enrollment boom, students born after 1981, known as the Millennial generation. Examines these students' attitudes, beliefs, and

behaviors, and makes recommendations to student affairs practitioners for working with them. Discusses historical and cultural influences that shape generations, demographics, teaching and learning patterns of Millennials, and how student affairs can best educate and serve them.
ISBN: 0-7879-7606-7

SS105   **Addressing the Unique Needs of Latino American Students**
Anna M. Ortiz
Explores the experiences of the fast-growing population of Latinos in higher education, and what these students need from student affairs. This volume examines the influence of the Latino family, socioeconomic levels, cultural barriers, and other factors to understand the challenges faced by Latinos. Discusses administration, student groups, community colleges, support programs, cultural identity, Hispanic-Serving Institutions, and more.
ISBN: 0-7879-7479-X

SS104   **Meeting the Needs of African American Women**
Mary F. Howard-Hamilton
Identifies and explores the critical needs for African American women as students, faculty, and administrators. This volume introduces theoretical frameworks and practical applications for addressing challenges; discusses identity and spirituality; explores the importance of programming support in recruitment and retention; describes the benefits of mentoring; and provides illuminating case studies of black women's issues in higher education.
ISBN: 0-7879-7280-0

SS103   **Contemporary Financial Issues in Student Affairs**
John H. Schuh
This volume addresses the challenging financial situation facing higher education and offers creative solutions for student affairs staff. Topics include the differences between public and private institutions in funding student activities, how to demonstrate financial accountability to stakeholders, plus ways to address budget challenges in student unions, health centers, campus recreation, counseling centers, and student housing.
ISBN: 0-7879-7173-1

SS102   **Meeting the Special Needs of Adult Students**
Deborah Kilgore, Penny J. Rice
This volume examines the ways student services professionals can best help adult learners. Chapters highlight the specific challenges that adult enrollment brings to traditional four-year and postgraduate institutions, which are often focused on the traditional-aged student experience. Explaining that adult students are typically involved in campus life in different ways than younger students are, the volume provides student services professionals with good guidance on serving an ever-growing population.
ISBN: 0-7879-6991-5

SS101   **Planning and Achieving Successful Student Affairs Facilities Projects**
Jerry Price
Provides student affairs professionals with an examination of critical facilities issues by exploring the experiences of their colleagues. Illustrates that students' educational experiences are affected by residence halls, student unions, dining services, recreation and wellness centers, and campus grounds, and that student affairs professionals make valuable contributions to the success of campus facility projects. Covers planning, budgeting, collaboration, and communication through case studies and lessons learned.
ISBN: 0-7879-6847-1

SS100   **Student Affairs and External Relations**
Mary Beth Snyder
Building positive relations with external constituents is as important in
student affairs work as it is in any other university or college division. This
issue is a long-overdue resource of ideas, strategies, and information aimed
at making student affairs leaders more effective in their interactions with
important off-campus partners, supporters, and agencies. Chapter authors
explore the current challenges facing the student services profession as well
as the emerging opportunities worthy of student affairs interest.
ISBN: 0-7879-6342-9

NEW DIRECTIONS FOR STUDENT SERVICES
Order Form
SUBSCRIPTIONS AND SINGLE ISSUES

DISCOUNTED BACK ISSUES:

*Use this form to receive **20% off** all back issues of New Directions for Student Services. All single issues priced at **$22.40** (normally $28.00)*

TITLE	ISSUE NO.	ISBN
_____	_____	_____
_____	_____	_____
_____	_____	_____

Call 888-378-2537 *or see mailing instructions below. When calling, mention the promotional code, JB7ND, to receive your discount.*

SUBSCRIPTIONS: *(1 year, 4 issues)*

☐ New Order   ☐ Renewal

U.S.	☐ Individual: $80	☐ Institutional: $195
Canada/Mexico	☐ Individual: $80	☐ Institutional: $235
All Others	☐ Individual: $104	☐ Institutional: $269

Call 888-378-2537 *or see mailing and pricing instructions below. Online subscriptions are available at www.interscience.wiley.com.*

Copy or detach page and send to:
John Wiley & Sons, Journals Dept, 5th Floor
989 Market Street, San Francisco, CA 94103-1741

Order Form can also be faxed to: 888-481-2665

Issue/Subscription Amount: $ _____	**SHIPPING CHARGES:**	
Shipping Amount: $ _____	SURFACE	Dometic Canadian
(for single issues only—subscription prices include shipping)	First Item	$5.00 $6.00
Total Amount: $ _____	Each Add'l Item	$3.00 $1.50

(No sales tax for U.S. subscriptions. Canadian residents, add GST for subscription orders. Individual rate subscriptions must be paid by personal check or credit card. Individual rate subscriptions may not be resold as library copies.)

☐ Payment enclosed (U.S. check or money order only. All payments must be in U.S. dollars.)

☐ VISA ☐ MC ☐ Amex # _____ Exp. Date _____

Card Holder Name _____ Card Issue # _____

Signature _____ Day Phone _____

☐ Bill Me (U.S. institutional orders only. Purchase order required.)

Purchase order # _____
Federal Tax ID13559302   GST 89102 8052

Name _____

Address _____

Phone _____ E-mail _____

NEW DIRECTIONS FOR STUDENT SERVICES IS NOW AVAILABLE ONLINE AT WILEY INTERSCIENCE

What is Wiley InterScience?

Wiley InterScience is the dynamic online content service from John Wiley & Sons delivering the full text of over 300 leading scientific, technical, medical, and professional journals, plus major reference works, the acclaimed *Current Protocols* laboratory manuals, and even the full text of select Wiley print books online.

What are some special features of Wiley InterScience?

Wiley InterScience Alerts is a service that delivers table of contents via e-mail for any journal available on Wiley InterScience as soon as a new issue is published online.
Early View is Wiley's exclusive service presenting individual articles online as soon as they are ready, even before the release of the compiled print issue. These articles are complete, peer-reviewed, and citable.
CrossRef is the innovative multi-publisher reference linking system enabling readers to move seamlessly from a reference in a journal article to the cited publication, typically located on a different server and published by a different publisher.

How can I access Wiley InterScience?

Visit http://www.interscience.wiley.com

Guest Users can browse Wiley InterScience for unrestricted access to journal Tables of Contents and Article Abstracts, or use the powerful search engine.
Registered Users are provided with a *Personal Home Page* to store and manage customized alerts, searches, and links to favorite journals and articles. Additionally, Registered Users can view free Online Sample Issues and preview selected material from major reference works.
Licensed Customers are entitled to access full-text journal articles in PDF, with select journals also offering full-text HTML.

How do I become an Authorized User?

Authorized Users are individuals authorized by a paying Customer to have access to the journals in Wiley InterScience. For example, a university that subscribes to Wiley journals is considered to be the Customer. Faculty, staff and students authorized by the university to have access to those journals in Wiley InterScience are Authorized Users. Users should contact their Library for information on which Wiley journals they have access to in Wiley InterScience.